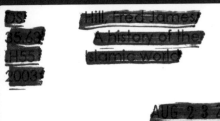

A History
of the
Islamic World

Illustrated Histories
from Hippocrene Books

A History
of the
Islamic World

Fred James Hill
&
Nicholas Awde

HIPPOCRENE BOOKS, INC.
NEW YORK

ILLUSTRATION CREDITS

Typeset & designed by Desert♥Hearts, London

ISBN 0-7818-1015-9

For information, address:
HIPPOCRENE BOOKS, INC.
171 Madison Avenue
New York, NY 10016
www.hippocrenebooks.com

Cataloging-in-Publication data available from
the Library of Congress

Printed in the United States of America.

Contents

List of Maps

Detail of a twelfth-century
lustered bowl, Cairo.

Foreword

The Islamic and Christian worlds together account for more than fifty percent of the world's estimated seven billion people. Sadly, despite enjoying a shared cultural and historical past, the political relationship between the two worlds is an uneasy one.

Boosted by the theory that a clash of civilizations is somehow inevitable, many consider that Islam has replaced Communism in recent decades as the major threat to the West's stability. A closer look behind the headlines reveals that in fact the majority of the West's current concerns with the Islamic world have existed in one form or another for many centuries. Furthermore, history reveals the existence of tensions not only between Islam and the Christian West, but also within the Islamic world. However, these constant flashpoints stemming from centuries-old disagreements detract from the parallel reality of peaceful and constructive co-existence.

We hope that this short history will go some way to explaining the historical contexts that have led to the complex situation today in the development of the Islamic world, standing at the dawn of the twenty-first century at the crossroads between tradition and modernity—the same position faced, with great turmoil, by the Christian world of the United States and Europe in the nineteenth and early twentieth centuries.

We also hope this book will highlight the diversity and extraordinary adaptability of one of the world's all-embracing cultures. For so many in the world, the institutions and culture of Islam have never ceased to be a source of inspiration and a pattern for progress. Islam is, after all, a religion that unites an international community with a way of life that reflects humankind from Morocco to China, from Kazan on the banks of the Volga to Fiji in the Pacific.

Fred James Hill &
Nicholas Awde

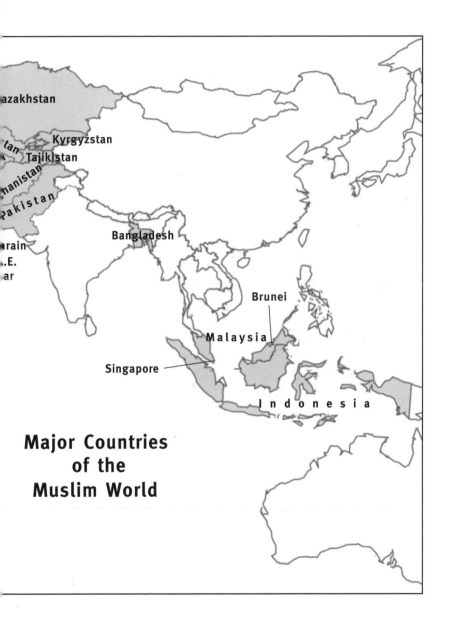

azakhstan

Kyrgyzstan
Tajikistan

hanista

akistan

rain
.E.
ar

Bangladesh

Brunei

Malaysia

Singapore

Indonesia

**Major Countries
of the
Muslim World**

Persian illuminated manuscript, depicting a scene from
the classic epic *Layla and Majnun*, 1530–31.

10

Introduction

*"Occidental culture was confined to its own little peninsulas:
Thomas Aquinas was read from Spain to Hungary and from Sicily
to Norway. But Ibn al-Arabi was read from Spain to Sumatra
and from the Swahili coast to Kazan on the Volga."*
—Marshall G. S. Hodgson, *The Venture of Islam*

Every day, around the world, hundreds of millions of people representing a myriad of ethnic groups and cultures turn to face a city in Saudi Arabia and recite verses from the Qur'an. Their focal point is Mecca, where the seventh-century Arab Prophet Muhammad destroyed images of pagan gods and urged his fellow humans to break with tradition and worship one God. Muhammad taught no less than Islam—"the surrender of the self to the will of God."

Within a matter of decades, his followers had established an empire that stretched from the borders of China in the east all the way to where the waves of the Atlantic Ocean lap the shores of Morocco, Spain, and Portugal. Today, after an eventful history spanning nearly 1,500 years, the religion remains a powerful and hugely influential force, with hardly a place in the world where its presence has not been felt.

While the Middle East continues to be the symbolic focus and spiritual heartland of Islam—as indeed it does for Christianity and Judaism—the religion has been long established in other regions of the world. Far from being merely an Arab religion, Islam is a multiracial, multicultural faith whose adherents speak many different languages.

The Arabs of the Middle East gave the world Islam, but a tradition of co-existence with the "Peoples of the Book"—those who respect the Old Testament—means that there are still significant and thriving Arab Christian populations across Egypt, Lebanon, Syria, and Iraq. And, throughout the ages, Arab identity has always been based on a shared history and common culture, the bonds of which were forged by the Arabic language. It is therefore important to point out here that not all Muslims are Arabs and that not all Arabs are Muslims.

Today, it is Indonesia that has the largest Muslim population in the

The Al-Azhar mosque and university in Cairo, one of the great spiritual centers of Sunni Islam.

world, a total of some two hundred million who make up more than ninety percent of the country. Islam has also enjoyed a centuries-old unbroken tradition in many other regions of Asia, as well as sub-Saharan Africa and parts of Europe, such as Bosnia-Herzogovina and Albania. Its continued vitality is attested by the fact that it has been steadily gaining ground in other parts of the world not traditionally associated with it, even becoming the fastest growing faith in the United States.

Of course, as with other religions, differences have always existed in Islam, and, like other religions, it has a wide range of mainstream and unorthodox denominations and sects, some of which do not necessarily sit well with each other. Rather than forming a monolithic political or economic power bloc in the world, the Islamic world also includes many competing Islamic nations and ethnic groups, along with the various social and economic divisions found in all parts of the world. Attempting to define a "typical" Islamic nation is, in fact, an impossible task. The responses to independence by the numerous Muslim-dominated nation-states that emerged in the post-colonial period have been varied, ranging from democratically based systems, featuring both secular and religious innovations, through to authoritarian or outright dictatorial regimes.

Meanwhile, in other states, such as Nigeria or India, where Muslims do not form a majority but have a long established presence, attempts have been made to adapt modern political systems with varying degrees of success. The inevitable collapse of the Soviet Union at the beginning of the 1990s created a whole batch of new Muslim-majority republics, including Uzbekistan and Azerbaijan, and with them a new set of challenges while, at the same time, Muslim regions such as Chechnya and Tatarstan have remained uneasily as autonomous entities within the Russian Federation, bringing in its wake further difficulties and dangers.

As this *History* will show, such transitions have never been easy at any period. Today, it is anti-Western resentment that characterizes the resistance of most Muslim nations to modern political change. But behind this lie reasons of widespread poverty and disenfranchisement among populations forced to remain in developing world conditions and tyrannical, corrupt regimes. Tackling problems such as these requires a united response by the Islamic world and the West and a decisive break with the all-too familiar pattern of rivalry and confrontation. An understanding of our shared history, which acknowledges the interdependence that has existed between Islam and the West and draws parallels between the age-old struggle for rights and freedom over the ages in both Islamic and Western societies, must surely help towards attaining this goal.

Islam's international outlook has not prevented it from being viewed generally in a negative light in the West, being perceived by many to be at odds with values that form the cornerstones of the Western world. More than anything else, the tragic events of September 11, 2001—committed by a group of terrorists claiming to act in the name of Islam—have brought the relationship of Islam and the rest of the global community into dramatically sharp relief. Yet such an act merely highlights the fact that, as with other religions too, Islam is no less vulnerable to being used by groups and individuals seeking to further their own political ends, a fact that is saddening to both Muslims and non-Muslims alike. The historical record does not support the commonly held image of a religion that is alien to and at odds with other faiths and beliefs—one that seeks to gain converts at all costs. The long history of Islam in fact affirms the value of partnership and linking world communities.

Indeed, at key stages in its existence, Islam has been at the forefront of world progress. While Europe was slumbering in the Dark Ages, the Islamic empires of the Umayyads, Fatimids and Al-

Minaret and mosque in Buhkara, present-day Uzbekistan.

Andalus—inheritors and guardians of the Greek and Roman body of learning—basked in the limelight, their cities famed throughout the known world as centers of cultural brilliance, enriching the world with its achievements in areas such as architecture, mathematics, astrology, medicine, and technology. Even when the nations of the West rose to prominence in later centuries, Islamic empires such as the Safavids, Mughals and Ottomans continued to make their mark firmly on the world map. And, far from keeping the rest of the world at bay, early Muslim traders created a network of trade routes that stretched across half of the globe, linking its diverse civilizations and cultures. Communication between these regions was through Arabic, the language of the Qur'an, which furthered religious and secular learning and facilitated the spread of ideas.

Another key aspect of Islam that is often overlooked is its intimate religious connection with the West. It is a faith that emerged from the same Middle Eastern cradle that gave the world its great monotheistic religions and it firmly acknowledges its Judeo-Christian roots. Along with Jews and Christians, Muslims venerate the major Old Testament prophets and worship the same God, called in Arabic "Allah"— meaning "The God"—while Jesus Christ ("Isa") and the Virgin Mary ("Maryam") hold their special place in Islam.

In fact, under Islamic law, the right of Christians and Jews to worship freely has long been protected, and history is full of examples that show this to have been put concretely into practice. Interestingly, while post-Medieval Christian Europe busied itself with stamping out religious nonconformity, hauling unfortunate victims before the Inquisition and pursuing heretics and Jews equally with horrific zeal, religious minorities were flourishing under the protection of Muslim governments such as the Ottoman Empire.

While it is not within the scope of this book to interpret the contents of the Qur'an, issues of a sensitive nature have been included, but treated from historical perspective, taking into account the consequences for non-Islamic communities. Controversies aside, first and foremost this book is a celebration of the history of a religious community that is full of surprises, drama, and wonder, and one that helps in equal measure to shed light on the world in which we all, regardless of creed, live.

The Rise of Islam

The forest of pillars filling the Mezquita in Cordoba, Spain. Work began on the mosque in the eighth century. It was later converted into a cathedral under the Christians.

GILLIAN JOYCE

The ancient city of Petra, today in Jordan, was strategically situated at the crossroads of several caravan routes that linked the lands of China, India, and South Arabia with the Mediterranean world. It was displaced by Palmyra in the second century A.D.

Cradle of Islam

"He was Caesar and Pope in one; but he was Pope
without Pope's pretensions, Caesar without the legions of Caesar:
without a standing army, without a bodyguard,
without a palace, without a fixed revenue."
—*Bosworth Smith* (Muhammad and Muhammadanism, *1874)*

The "Age of Ignorance"—or *Jahiliyya*—is the name given by Muslims to the time before Islam was made known by their Prophet Muhammad in the seventh century A.D. The setting for arrival of such a profound message was the Arabian Peninsula, which, except for fertile lands in the south, is a huge expanse of mostly barren desert and mountain terrain, covering an area roughly a third the size of the U.S.A. Towards the south lies a geographical wonder known as the Empty Quarter, the largest active sand-sea on earth, which covers an area larger than France.

Difficult though the conditions were in the Arabian Peninsula around the period when Muhammad lived, it was far from uninhabited. A group of nomadic and sedentary tribes known as the Bedouin had developed qualities and skills that enabled them to thrive in the region. More than this, their familiarity with the terrain and inter-tribal organization allowed them to control major trade routes that passed through the Peninsula, linking it with Syria, Persia, East Africa and India, providing caravans with animals, guides, and guards. A wide variety of goods were transported including incense, such as frankincense and myrrh, spices, gold, ivory, pearls, precious stones, and textiles. Descendants of these same Bedouin tribes can still be found in the region, and their way of life is remarkably unchanged from the days of Muhammad.

Adjacent to Arabia lay two of the great rival superpowers of the day—the Byzantine and Sassanian Empires. Together, they dominated a huge swathe of territory stretching from Eastern Europe across the Middle East and into parts of Central Asia and which encompassed some of the greatest trade routes of the day. The Christian Byzantine Empire was the eastern part of the former Roman Empire, which for political and religious reasons had split into two. The Holy Emperors of Byzantium ruled from their capital of Constantinople (today Istanbul in Turkey), lording over the lands of the eastern Mediterranean. Meanwhile, to the east, the Sassanian Empire dominated Persia and surrounding territories, its kings wielding power from their capital at Ctesiphon (near present-day Baghdad). The Sassanians were strict adherents of Zoroastrianism, the official state religion that had long been associated with Persia and which was characterized by monotheistic leanings, a firm belief in a universal struggle of good and evil, and a special emphasis on fire rituals.

Continuously at odds with each other, the two superpowers vied for control of the surrounding regions and their lucrative trade routes. This they did either by brute force or by expertly exploiting local religious and ethnic rivalries. Caught up in the struggle for economic supremacy was the region of Arabia.

Traders in the Arabian Heartland

The Quraysh were a tribe of Arabian traders who found themselves in a particularly enviable position. Good fortune had brought prosperous trade that once passed through the ancient and great cities of Petra (today in Jordan) and Palmyra (in Syria) into their hands. Making its way down the western side of the peninsula—a fertile strip called the Hijaz that contrasted with the harsh deserts to the east—it now passed through their stronghold of Mecca. By the end of the sixth century, their handling of international trade en route from Yemen to Syria, and from Abyssinia to Iraq, and beyond, had made them extremely prosperous.

Getting caravans of consumer goods safely through their arduous and dangerous trans-Arabian journey required inventive and skillful management, a task the Quraysh excelled in. Using their insider knowledge of the Arabian Peninsula and its customs, they made pacts with local tribes to secure safe passage for the caravans as well as striking deals with their own traders with both the Byzantine and Sassanian authorities. In fact, the Quraysh were fast becoming victims of their own success, growing wealthier while other tribes grew ever

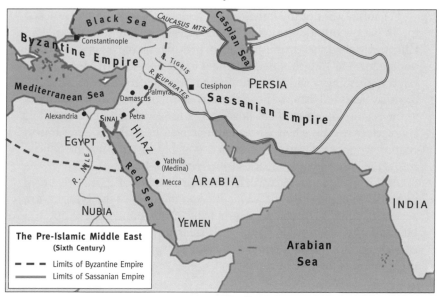

The Pre-Islamic Middle East
(Sixth Century)
– – – Limits of Byzantine Empire
═══ Limits of Sassanian Empire

envious of their privileged position, a dangerous situation to be in given the fractious tribal politics of Arabia.

Underpinning the trade system was religion. Mecca itself, though an extremely busy marketplace controlled by the Quraysh, had long been a major pilgrim center for a variety of traditional faiths. It was home to a shrine known as the Ka'aba (from the Arabic meaning "cube"), a windowless stone cubic structure which, reflecting the region's Biblical heritage, was traditionally held to have been built by Adam and then rebuilt by Abraham. Set in one of its corners is the Black Stone (Hajar), a piece of rock (possibly a meteorite) said to have been given to Abraham by the Archangel Gabriel.

Within the Ka'aba were also housed numerous gods, placed there by the different tribes that inhabited Arabia. Every year, a long truce allowed pilgrims from around the peninsula to visit their gods here—a time of peace that brought pilgrims, poets, and orators flocking into the region. The sacred area surrounding the Ka'aba was designated a sanctuary where violence and the carrying of weapons were absolutely forbidden. Disarmed and with their safety guaranteed, the Arab tribesmen were able to temporarily put aside their grievances and vendettas and get on with the business of trading and cultural exchange.

Paganism was not the only form of religion that Mecca was exposed to. In fact, both of the great monotheistic religions, Judaism and Christianity, had also established a firm presence on the peninsula. In the trading town of Yathrib, some 320 miles to the northeast of Mecca, there was a flourishing Jewish community that would feature prominently in the early years of Islam, while in the very south of the Arabian Peninsula in the region of Yemen there flourished a Jewish kingdom. Although it is not clear exactly when Christianity arrived in Arabia, by the fourth century it too was clearly in existence, possibly having been introduced across the desert by missionaries from Syria and Iraq.

And so it was into this world that the Prophet of Islam was born, in Mecca in approximately A.D. 570. As a member of the Hashimites, a clan belonging to the Quraysh tribe, Muhammad grew up in a bustling city where merchants with their different gods and beliefs converged, bringing in their wake great prosperity, and stories of the great empires that lay beyond.

The Life of Muhammad

Compared with prophets of the world's other great religions, such as Jesus, Buddha and Zoroaster, Muhammad's life is remarkably well documented. Very early in Islamic history, Muslim scholars began to examine and reexamine his life in an attempt to gain as faithful a picture as possible. A huge amount of importance is attached his actions and deeds, deemed in Islam to be exemplary and lived in accordance with the message of God. Thus, while Islamic dogma stresses Muhammad's human nature, his example is held as a model for all Muslims to conduct their own lives.

Muhammad's early life was marked by the tragic loss of both his parents by the tender age of six. The task of caring for the orphan first fell to his grandfather and then to his uncle Abu Talib, a merchant. Under his uncle's guidance, Muhammad learned the ins and outs of trade, going on trips as far as Syria that gave him first-hand knowledge of other cultures and religions. During the course of his early career in commerce, Muhammad began to earn a great deal of respect among the trading community on account of his hard work and fairness.

When he was in his mid-twenties, he married Khadija, a widow some fifteen years his senior. She was a wealthy merchant in her own right who had employed him to look after her caravan trade, and

The Ka'aba in Mecca is the center of the circumambulations performed by pilgrims during the Hajj pilgrimage and it is toward the Ka'aba that Muslims face in their prayers wherever they are. The Black Stone, possibly of meteoric origin, is located at one of its outside corners. Around the Ka'aba is a restricted area, or "haram," extending in some directions as far as 12 miles, which only Muslims may enter.

together they had several children including a daughter named Fatima, whose eventual marriage to Muhammad's cousin Ali would be a highly significant event in the development of Islam. During Khadija's lifetime, Muhammad married no other woman, but after her death in 619 at the age of sixty-five, he would go on to take other wives, for the most part to cement ties of loyalty and to provide for the well-being of the widows of fallen warriors.

Muhammad was greatly given to contemplation and regularly took to retiring to a cave high on a mountain above Mecca, where he would sit for long periods in solitude and reflection. It was here, in 610, at the age of approximately forty years, that he received the first of many revelations. Confronted by the Archangel Gabriel ("Jibril," the same as in the Old Testament), Muhammad, who could not read or write, was commanded to recite the first words of the Qur'an, the Holy Scripture of Islam, which had appeared before him on a silk cloth with fiery writing. This marked the beginning of a period lasting more than twenty years during which the entire contents of the Qur'an would be revealed to Muhammad verse by verse.

The Family of the Prophet

The marriages of the Prophet Muhammad were for a variety of reasons: some from personal affinity, some to widows who had no one to turn to, while others were politically motivated to create or maintain alliances. He was not married to all of his wives at the same time.

They are, in chronological order:

1) In the early part of his life Muhammad had only one wife, **Khadija** (556–619). She was a wealthy merchant woman and he had worked as master of her caravans before marrying her around 595, when she was between 40 and 45. She died at age 65 and was the first to believe in the Prophet's Mission.

2) After her death he married a Quraysh woman, **Sauda bint Zam'a** (596–674), in 631 when she was 35. She was the widow of Sakran, one of the Companions.

3) **Aisha** (614–678) was Abu Bakr's daughter. She was six when wed and the marriage was only later consummated when in 623/624 she came of age.

4) **Hafsa**, 18, was the daughter of Umar bin al-Khattab and the widow of Khunais. She recently had returned with other Muslim exiles from Abyssinia and married Muhammad in 625. Born in 607, she is reported in various accounts as having died in 647/648, 661/662 or 665.

5) **Zainab bint Khuzaima** was a widow of Ubaida. She was known as "Umm al-Masakin" or "Mother of the Poor" on account of her generosity. Born in 595, she died soon after the marriage in 626 at the age of 31.

6) **Umm Salama** (598/599–682/3), the widow of Abu Salama

7) **Zainab bint Jahsh**, 40, the divorced wife of the Prophet's adopted son Zaid. She died in 640/641 at the age of between 50 and 53.

8) **Juwairiyya bint Harith** (605–670) was the daughter of the chief of the Musta'liq tribe.

9) **Umm Habiba** (591–665) was the widow of Ubaid and the daughter of Abu Sufyan, the leader of the Meccans who opposed Muhammad. They were married by proxy while she was still in Abyssinia.

10) **Safiyya** (628–670 or 672), married at 17 in 628, was the widow of Kinana, chief of the Jews of Khaibar.

11) **Maimuna** (602–681), the sister of Abbas and a widow, was married to Muhammad when she was 51.

The Prophet also had at least two concubines:

1) **Raihana**, a Jew taken captive from the Qurayza tribe.

2) **Marya**, a Christian slave who was a gift from the ruler of Egypt.

Khadija was the only wife to bear the Prophet children—two (perhaps three) sons: **Qasim** and **Abdullah** (or Tahir), who all died in infancy; and four daughters: **Umm Kulthum, Ruqayya, Zainab** and **Fatima**. They all married, but Umm Kulthum and Ruqayya died before their father. Marya was the mother of the Prophet's son **Ibrahim**, who died when he was two.

So inspired, he began to publicly preach a set of beliefs that were considered heretical by many at the time and constituted the blueprint for a religious, political, and social revolution—striking at the very structures that underpinned the power of the dominant Quraysh. Muhammad entreated his fellow Meccans to do no less than to cast aside their pagan beliefs and worship one God alone—the very same worshipped by their fellow Jews and Christians. He also condemned the ethos, firmly embraced by the Quraysh, of single-mindedly pursuing wealth and ignoring any consideration of their social responsibilities to the less well-off. He insisted that all had an obligation to take care of the poor, weak, and orphaned. A practice he found particularly abhorrent was that of female infanticide, which was widespread in pre-Islamic Arabia. So as to avoid the taboo of spilling the blood of a relation, these infant girls were buried alive in the desert.

Muhammad's message was one that Meccans had little to desire to accept, and during the course of some thirteen long, hard years, he gained more enemies than he had supporters. Yet he did have a number of dedicated followers made up of a close circle of family and friends, including his wife Khadija—considered Islam's very first convert.

Whatever the consequences, Muhammad refused to stop preaching his message. And so, faced with growing unpopularity and a serious threats, his position in Mecca eventually became untenable and he had little option but to abandon the city. Accordingly, in 622, Muhammad and his followers sought refuge in the town of Yathrib. Known as the Hijra ("Migration"), the event is of major significance in Islam and it is from this date that the first year in the Islamic calendar begins.

The Birth of the Islamic State

The choice of Yathrib was no mere coincidence. Muhammad had already gained a number of converts there over the years, known as the "Helpers" or "Ansar," and it was they who would give support and help to the dispossessed newcomers, dubbed the "Emigrants" or "Muhajirs," who belonged for the most part to Muhammad's own Hashimite clan. Furthermore, with a known reputation for fairness and sound judgment, Muhammad found himself invited to act as mediator in the complex disputes that had arisen in the city amongst

The Islamic Faith

"There is no God but God and Muhammad is the Prophet of God"

The religion preached by Muhammad is founded on the central tenet that there is one God, Allah, around which are a set of beliefs and rituals that together create a powerful sense of religious community. The word "Islam" itself means literally "submission," a reflection of the doctrine of submission to God.

At the heart of Islam lies the Qur'an, the sacred book of Islam. For Muslims the Qur'an is no less than the word of God, revealed to the Prophet Muhammad through the Angel Gabriel. Since the Qur'an is considered to be the exact word of God, it is held that translations into other languages, although serving a purpose, cannot render its true meaning. Thus Muslims everywhere strive to learn it in its original Arabic form. This fact also played a major part in the use of Arabic as a lingua franca which helped create strong cultural links among the very different cultures that make up the Islamic World.

Initially memorized by Muhammad, who did not read or write, and some of his most trusted followers, the Qur'an was first written down shortly after the Prophet's death on a wide variety of materials such as scraps of parchment, leather, tablets of stone, and even the shoulder bones of animals.

Central to the practice of Islam are the Five Pillars:

■ **Shahada**—the act of publicly testifying that "there is no god but God and Muhammad is the messenger of God."

■ **Salat**—the act of praying five times a day and, if free, attending congregational prayers on Friday.

■ **Zakat**—the obligation, not choice, of giving a proportion of one's wealth to charity.

■ **Sawm**—fasting during the holy month of Ramadan.

■ **Hajj**—making the pilgirimage to Mecca during the second week of Dhu 'l-Hijja, the twelfth month of the Muslim calendar, at least once in one's lifetime provided it is within one's means to do so.

The pilgrimage to Mecca is a powerful institution which has always had a profound effect on Muslims. It is here that they come into contact with other believers from all over the world—a tremendous mix of ethnic groups speaking a multitude of languages, which reinforces for them the universal nature of the religion. The focal point in Mecca is the Ka'aba, which is covered by a huge black cloth adorned with gold lettering, although its importance is symbolic, and it is not an object of worship.

To become a Muslim one should declare the Shahada in front of witnesses. The act of renouncing the Islamic faith is taken extremely seriously, and it has tradionally held that male apostates should, under certain circumstances, be put to death—yet there are many Muslims who reject such a response and the subject has been the source of a great deal of debate within Islam.

Islam and the Old Testament

Muhammad did not only stage a religious revolution against the paganism of the Meccans. While he made no claim to have invented the religion of Islam, he made it clear that he had received a direct revelation from the very same God of the Bible, i.e. the Old Testament or Torah. He was therefore "confirming" the scriptures in accordance with God's wishes. For this reason there was also a clear message for the Christians and the Jews: they had strayed from the true path which had now been revealed in the Qur'an.

Yet, rather than compelling them to convert, the Qur'an is highly respectful of the Jewish and Christian Biblical traditions. While Muslims hold that Muhammad is the greatest and final Prophet, they also hold that God had provided a succession of prophets before him, including Noah ("Nuh"), Abraham ("Ibrahim"), Moses ("Musa"), David ("Dawud"), Solomon ("Sulayman"), and Jesus ("Isa"). Their mission was to guide the world and convey the message of Islam, the surrendering of the will to God.

Jesus, who is mentioned many times in the Qur'an, is a highly revered figure in Islam, and is considered one of the greatest prophets after Muhammad himself. They do not attribute any divine qualities to Jesus, but regard him as entirely human by nature. Muslims believe that Jesus' life has been misrepresented in the Christian scriptures. They do not, for instance, believe that he died to redeem the sins of the world, nor do they agree with the Christian version of events surrounding the Crucifixion. They hold, instead, that Jesus was killed not by the Romans or Jews, but that he was carried up to heaven and another person resembling him was put to death in his place. Islam, which maintains the concept of the Virgin Birth, also accords great respect to Jesus' mother Mary ("Maryam"), also mentioned in the Qur'an.

In Islam there are no priests and the hierarchy typically seen in Christianity is absent—all Muslims are considered on a spiritually equal footing and any is entitled to lead congregational prayers. Yet Muslim communities have always given a great deal of importance to scholars, or Ulema, who interpret the laws of Islam, which led to the growth of a highly powerful body of theologians worldwide. However, this reliance on the sometimes conflictive judgment of others obviously runs certain risks, and such empowerment in clerics has on many occasions created opportunities for individuals and groups wishing to exploit their privileged position for political or personal gain.

the Arabs and the three Jewish tribes—the Qaynuga, Nadir, and Qurayza—over control of the city's resources and wealth.

Addressing the problem, Muhammad set about consulting with the different communities of Yathrib in an attempt to forge a unified community, governed by laws that were acceptable to all and in accordance with the spirit of his revelations. The fruit of his endeavor was a simple constitution which the three main groups—the Ansar (Muslims native to Yathrib), the Muhajirs (the immigrants from Mecca) and the Jews—agreed to accept as binding.

Under the new laws, each group was entitled to practice its religion freely and enjoyed a fair degree of autonomy, but with clearly identified responsibilities to the community. Only when disputes could not be resolved satisfactorily at a local level would Muhammad himself step in and pass judgment. However, all matters relating to the overall security of the community, such as war and relations with the Quraysh in Mecca, were to be dealt with exclusively by the Prophet. And so Yathrib swiftly became known as "Medina" (from *Madinat al-Nabi*, or the "City of the Prophet").

While Muhammad's position as a political and religious leader went from strength to strength, he nevertheless maintained a life of asceticism. Living a humble existence, he was said to have had only one change of clothes which he mended himself. While Muslims proudly talk of his compassion and love for people, they do not forget that he was also a highly astute politician and military commander, praised for the diplomacy and bravery with which he actively sought to change the politics and social organization of the world in which he lived, in accordance with the new principles of Islam.

The community he established in his own lifetime in Yathrib/Medina is held to be an ideal example of the Islamic state. During this time Muhammad also continued to receive revelations, which formed the basis of his legal rulings. It was also during this period that the Islamic ban on intoxicants and gambling was established, and that laws against murder, theft, and adultery were revealed to Muhammad and accordingly defined.

Muhammad Returns to Mecca

It was not long before the Muslims, consolidating their position in the favorable conditions offered by Medina, began to clash with the still-hostile Meccans. A major confrontation took place in 624 after the Muslims set out to intercept a caravan carrying a great deal of valuable goods from Palestine to Mecca. In an attempt to crush the Muslims, the Meccans promptly dispatched a large force of a thousand armed men. Outnumbered three to one, the Muslims won the ensuing conflict, and carried home the spoils of war. The Battle of Badr, as it became known, proved to be a turning point—Islam had shown itself to be more than a religious movement, and was now a political and military force to be reckoned with.

While the Muslims had mixed results over the next few years in their military ventures, Muhammad's standing as a leader increased with the Bedouin tribes of the peninsula. Although the Muslims lost the Battle of Uhud against the Meccans in 625, they continued to stand up to Mecca and grew in strength. In 627, at the Battle of the Trench, the Muslims were successful in resisting a major campaign by the Meccans and their allies to invade Medina. On this occasion, on Muhammad's orders, the Muslims built a ditch around their city and after a two-week siege the attackers withdrew. In 629, after he successfully concluded a treaty with the Meccans, Muhammad and some followers were able to make a pilgrimage to the holy sites of Mecca.

The Battle of the Trench coincided with an incident that remains the source of considerable controversy. The discovery of a plot in support of the Meccans amongst the Jewish Qurayza tribe led to a major Muslim assault on the Jews back in Medina. On their surrender the men—between 600 and 900—were executed while the women and children were sold into slavery.

Prior to this, there had been a distancing between the two communities. Muhammad had already expelled the Jewish Qaynuga and Nadir tribes from Medina. Furthermore, Muslims also had begun to adopt new rituals. In 624, Muhammad had received a revelation instructing him that Muslims should no longer face Jerusalem during prayers, a practice they had shared with the Jews. From then onwards, Muslims would turn in the direction of Mecca. Furthermore, Muhammad, informed again by divine revelation, instructed the Muslims not to fast any more on Yom Kippur, the Jewish Day of Atonement, but to fast during the whole of the month of Ramadan.

Undeterred by the infighting, however, Muhammad continued with his long-term strategy until 630, when the moment the Prophet

The Islamic Calendar

The Islamic *hijri* year is based on the cycles of the moon, divided into twelve lunar (synodic) months of twenty-nine or thirty days, each of which is calculated according to the period between one new moon—*hilal*, the first sighting of the crescent—and the next. The year is approximately 354 days long, making it ten or eleven days shorter than a solar year. Dates of the Muslim calendar therefore have no fixed relationship either to dates of the Western (Gregorian) calendar or to the seasons of the year.

The lunar system was first introduced in 638 by the second Caliph, Umar. He did it in an attempt to rationalize the various, often conflicting, dating systems used at the time. After much consultation on the starting date of the new Islamic calendar, it was finally agreed that the most appropriate event was the Hijra—the migration of the Prophet Muhammad from Mecca to Medina in 622, and the central historical event of early Islam. The actual starting date for the calendar was chosen (on the basis of purely lunar years, counting backwards) to be the first day of the first month (1 Muharram) of the year of the Hijra.

Muslims call the Gregorian calendar *miladi* ("birth"), referring to the birth of Jesus Christ. The *hijri* calendar is usually abbreviated in Western languages as A.H.—from the Latin *Anno Hegirae* or "in the year of the Hijra." Muharram 1, 1 A.H., therefore corresponds to July 16, 622 A.D. The Islamic year consists of twelve lunar months:

1) Muharram (30 days)
2) Safar (29 days)
3) Rabi' al-Awwal (30 days)
4) Rabi' al-Thani (29 days)
5) Jumada 'l-Awwal (30 days)
6) Jumada 'l-Thani (29 days)
7) Rajab (30 days)
8) Sha'ban (29 days)
9) Ramadan (30 days)
10) Shawwal (29 days)
11) Dhu 'l-Qa'da (30 days)
12) Dhu 'l-Hijja (29 days; 30 in leap years)

Iran, Afghanistan, Kudistan, and parts of Central Asia also use the ancient Zoroastrian "Persian" solar (or *shamsi*) year (often all three systems are used at the same time). The twelve months of the Persian year follow the Gregorian year, but the numbering begins with the year of the Hijra. The year 2000, therefore, is 1420/1421 in Islamic years and 1379 in Persian years.

Ramadan is the month of fasting and **Dhu 'l-Hijja** the month of the Hajj pilgrimage to Mecca. The most important festivals in the Islamic year include **Id al-Fitr**, the "Little Feast" when the Ramadan fast is broken; and **Id al-Adha**, the "Great Feast" that celebrates the Hajj.

A popular festival is the **Mawlid**, or Birthday, of the Prophet (Rabi' al-Awwal 12). **Ashura** (Muharram 10) is when Shi'is celebrate the martyrdom of Ali's son Husayn.

Muslims in Turkey, Iran, Kurdistan, Afghanistan, and the republics of the Caucasus and Central Asia also celebrate **Now-Ruz**, the "Persian" New Year, on March 20-21.

and his followers had waited for finally arrived. Assembling a large force, they were able to their sights on the city that had not so long ago made outcasts of them. In what proved to be an almost bloodless act, the Muslims entered Mecca without opposition, led by Muhammad mounted on a camel. In fact, the only fatalities, reportedly eleven in all, occurred during a skirmish outside the city. In an act of reconciliation, Muhammad declared an amnesty and spared the Meccans and their families, property and businesses.

Mecca now would be changed for good. Muhammad immediately set about destroying the pagan gods in the Ka'aba, fulfilling his great mission to restore the shrine to the monotheism of "Abraham." Meccans were required to adopt Islam and their city was converted into the holiest city in Islam, its access forbidden to all but the faithful. To this day, all Muslims are called on to make a pilgrimage ("Hajj") to Mecca at a special time of the year at least once in their lifetime—if it is within their means to do so—an act that fulfills one of the Five Pillars of Islam.

Under Muhammad's leadership, the Muslims had now become a major force on the Arabian Peninsula, and tribes from the region sought out the Prophet to offer him their allegiance. A series of campaigns soon reined in most of those who continued to resist the new religious movement.

In 632, after a brief illness, Islam's great Prophet died. He was buried on the same spot where he died, at the house of his third and favorite wife, Aisha. Today his grave in Medina remains a place of devoted pilgrimage.

Muhammad's death left the Muslim community in a profound state of shock. Apart from the grief at the loss of their Prophet (many had believed the world would end with his death), Muslims had to come to terms with the fact that he had left no instructions as to who should succeed him, leaving the community adrift without a leader. The decision would be now be left entirely to them and it would become one of the most divisive issues in the history of Islam, the consequences of which still are keenly felt to this day.

The Arab Conquests
and the
Age of Empire

*"When they had subjugated the populations of the lands they conquered,
they employed them in their households as servants and craftsmen, choosing
the ablest—they soon learned from them how to change their ways.
Nay, they even pushed things to the point of refinement."
—Ibn Khaldun, thirteenth-century historian, writing on the
Arab Conquests* (Muqaddima)

The Early Years—A Crisis of Leadership

The years immediately following the death of Muhammad proved an extremely formative period. They set the scene for the emergence of the first great Muslim dynasty of the Umayyads, which would oversee the creation of a huge Islamic empire. Yet it was also a time of great bloodshed and treachery. Turning their weapons against each other, Muhammad's followers fought bitterly over the leadership of the Muslim community. The problems proved insurmountable, spawning rival lineages and a permanent rift that remains today.

Muhammad had created a community where religion, not tribal blood ties, was the basis upon which people identified with each other. The challenge now facing the Muslims was not only who might legitimately lead their community, but also what form the leadership should take. Clearly no other could take Muhammad's place since he was held to be the final Prophet. In the uncertainty of the new world that was rapidly emerging before them, the Muslims were caught between the traditional Arab government (nominating elders by tribal consensus) and the need for a new form of leadership that could respond to the demands of an expanding new state that was to be populated by Arabs and non-Arabs, Muslims and non-Muslims alike.

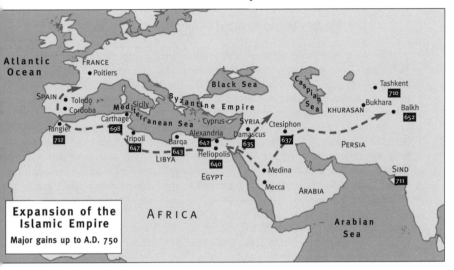

Atlantic Ocean

FRANCE
• Poitiers

Black Sea

Tashkent
710

SPAIN
• Toledo
• Cordoba
Med
Sicily
Byzantine Empire
KHURASAN
Bukhara
Balkh
652

Carthage
erranean Sea
Cyprus
SYRIA
Ctesiphon

Tangier
698
Tripoli
647
Barqa
643
642
Alexandria
Damascus
635
637
PERSIA

Heliopolis
640
LIBYA

EGYPT
Medina

Mecca
ARABIA

712

711
SIND

Expansion of the Islamic Empire

Major gains up to A.D. 750

AFRICA

Arabian Sea

Immediately after Muhammad's death, it seemed natural that four of his close followers would take charge of the community. Elected by the Arab tradition, they came to be referred to as Caliphs, or "khalifas," a term meaning "successors" or "deputies" of Muhammad, the Messenger of God.

Four leaders—Abu Bakr (r. 632-634), Umar (634-644), Uthman (644-56) and Ali (656-61)—successively ruled during a period that is looked upon by orthodox Muslims, or "Sunnis," as the Golden Age of the "Rightly Guided Caliphs." Each of these had known Muhammad personally and so his transmitted authority uniquely gave them the respect and loyalty of the growing number of Muslims under their rule.

However, a significant faction of Muslims refused to accept the legitimacy of the first three leaders. They believed that Muhammad had given a number of indications that Ali, who in fact became the Fourth Caliph and was the Prophet's cousin and son-in-law, was the sole legitimate successor and was therefore to head the community after Muhammad's death—a claim rejected by the Sunni Muslims. This argument of succession also held that the descendants of Ali and his wife, Muhammad's daughter Fatima, were similarly destined to lead the community. Ali's supporters therefore became known as the Shi'is (also Shi'a or Shi'tes)—from *Shi'at Ali* meaning "Ali's party."

This division in Islam had both political and religious consequences. It led to a civil war between the Muslims, during the

The Muslim World Divided—Sunnism versus Shi'ism

Of all the different non-orthodox Islamic denominations, the Shi'is remain the largest—with adherents spread around the world, in addition to their stronghold of Iran. Tensions between them and the "orthodox" Sunnis have at times resulted in bloodshed, the result of a bitter rift between the two sides that developed in the early years of Islamic history.

The causes of the schism lay in a dispute over how the community should be led after the death of Muhammad, who had left no clear successor. In an attempt to fill the void, a line of elected Caliphs was established: Abu Bakr, Umar and Uthman. The choice of the fourth Caliph, Ali, Muhammad's cousin and son-in-law, proved to be a flashpoint. Civil war broke out as the Prophet's widow Aisha and her supporters challenged Ali's accession to the Caliphate. Although Ali secured a massive victory against her at the Battle of the Camel (656, near Basra, Iraq), the matter was never resolved. Rejecting outright the legitimacy of the first three Caliphs, Ali's supporters closed ranks and established an enduring movement within Islam that became known as the Shi'is (from *Shi'at Ali* meaning "Ali's party," or "partisans of Ali"). The Shi'is would always maintain that Muhammad had named Ali his successor, and that the descendants of Ali were therefore the rightful heirs to the Caliphate.

Ali met a violent end at the hands of an assassin in 661, a mere five years into his rule as Caliph. His killer was another dissenter, one of the "Kharijis," a group that had withdrawn its support for Ali. His archrival Mu'awiya seized the advantage to step in as Caliph. However, Mu'awiya was careful to secure the backing of Ali's son, Hasan, who had relinquished his own claims to the leadership. Yet the Shi'is never accepted the legitimacy of the Umayyads, the hereditary dynasty founded by Mu'awiya. Hasan died in 680—perhaps poisoned—and civil war broke out yet again as his younger brother Husayn led a revolt that year against Yazid, the next Caliph. The uprising led to the massacre of Husayn and his supporters at the Battle of Karbala in 680, in Iraq. He was shot through the mouth with an arrow, a troop of Yazid's horsemen then rode back and forth over Husayn's body, and his head was carried in triumph from the battlefield. It is an event Shi'is consider the greatest of tragedies and is commemorated every year during the festival of Ashura, when zealous devotees are moved to whip themselves as they lament Husayn's martyrdom. Today, Karbala is a major Shi'i pilgrim center, attracting millions annually from all over the world.

Meanwhile, the majority of Muslims—the "orthodox" Sunnis—continued to maintain the legitimacy of the first four Caliphs, of which Ali was but one. The Sunnis also generally lent their support to subsquent incarnations of the institution of the Caliphate, headed by hereditary dynasties. During the first few hundred years they would wield an enormous degree of political power over the Islamic Empire firstly from Damascus and then Baghdad. Under these Caliphs the orthodox body of laws and traditions was developed into what it is today. While the Caliphate experienced a decline in political power, and the Caliphs became mere figureheads, the institution provided an important role as a banner for

Azerbaijani Shi'i Muslims celebrating Ashura in Baku, Azerbaijan, in the early twentieth century.

orthodox religious unity, and highly controversial claims to the role ensured its survival up until the 1920s.

Always a minority, the Shi'is had to satisfy themselves with a subordinate role in the Islamic world. They established their own rival dynasty of "Imams," descended from Ali and Fatima, and adhered to a quite distinct interpretation of Islam that is firmly rejected by Sunnis. The Shi'i Shahada, or declaration of faith, states: "There is no god but Allah, Muhammad is the Messenger of Allah, Ali is the Friend of Allah, the Successor of the Messenger of Allah and his First Caliph." The Shi'is steadfastly maintained that the leadership of the Sunni dynasties was an aberration, stained by tyranny and corruption. Yet they remained generally undecided as to how they should proceed in their dealings with Sunnis, and disagreements over this and other issues developed within their own ranks, eventually giving rise to a split in the line of Imams.

The most influential group of Shi'is, known as the "Twelvers," venerate twelve Imams in all, believing them to have been chosen by God and to be infallible. The final Imam was believed to have mysteriously disappeared in 873. From that time, the Twelvers began a long wait for his return as the "Mahdi" or "Messiah," and for the occasion when he would avenge the wrongdoings perpetrated against them by the more numerous Sunnis and restore justice in the prelude to the Last Judgment. Until the Twelfth Imam's return, it was the Shi'is lot to suffer unjust rulers and their corrupt governments. To enable them to cope with the wider Muslim community, they practiced "taqiya," which permitted them in times of danger to conceal their true beliefs, and melt into the mainstream and conform. The rebellion would wait until the coming of the Mahdi.

Another significant group is the Ismailis, also known as the Seveners, who split over the recognition of the Seventh Imam. Most Ismailis recognize the Aga Khan as the representative on earth of their hidden Imam.

course of which Sunnism would establish itself as the dominant force in Islam, leaving the minority Shi'is with a long-lasting sense of bitterness towards the orthodox majority.

Despite the fractious politics of the time, the armies of the Arab Muslims had already begun to push out of the confines of the Arabian Peninsula, launching major campaigns into neighboring regions and scoring significant gains for the fledgling Islamic state. In 635, the Arabs seized Damascus in Syria, and two years later the holy city of Jerusalem. As early as 633, booty-seeking Arab armies had begun to enter Persia and in 642 a major Arab military expedition delivered a massive blow the Persian army, sealing the fate of the already crumbling Sassanian Empire.

To the west, in the winter of 639 an Arab army stormed into the Byzantine territory of Egypt from Syria and, reinforced by troops from various Arab tribes, secured victories along the Nile, seizing the prized Mediterranean port of Alexandria in September 642. Moving west along the north coast of Africa, the Arabs also captured Barqa in 643, and Tripoli in 643-647 (both in present-day Libya). Finally, in 661 the Muslims transferred their capital to Damascus and established a new dynasty that would transform the Islamic state into a true empire.

The Empire of the Umayyads

With the creation of the first great Arab dynasty of the Umayyads (r. 661 to 750), Islamic power would adopt an aura of invincibility. For the next century Islamic history would be dominated by the dramatic campaigns of unstoppable Muslim Arab conquest. Using Damascus as their new capital, the Umayyad Caliphs stamped their authority across a huge empire that at its peak clawed at the borders of China in the east and sprawled west along North Africa to the shores of the Atlantic and up into Spain.

It was Mu'awiya, Ali's successor as Caliph, who engineered the move to Damascus. Transferring the Caliphate was a highly significant event, marking the end of the Arabian Peninsula's role as the base of Muslim political power—although being home to Mecca and Medina, it would never lose its importance as the spiritual home of Islam.

With the establishment of the capital in Damascus, a wealthy city that was once part of the Christian Byzantine Empire, an entirely new concept of caliphal leadership developed, influenced by the imperial world which the Arabs had stepped into. Whereas under the rule of the Four Rightly Guided Caliphs, Islam's supreme leaders had been elected according to social convention and limited themselves to the political sphere, the Umayyad Caliphs began to claim substantially more powers for themselves.

Breaking with tradition, Mu'awiya attempted to establish the Caliphate along the lines of the hereditary principle by nominating his son Yazid as his successor. The bid sparked off a new civil war, but the determined Caliph got his way in the end, setting a precedent that would continue for centuries, allowing the role of Caliph to be passed down the family line. Backed by their jurists, the Umayyad Caliphs began to put forward controversial theories of kingship that had little to do with Arab tradition and even less with Islam. No longer merely political leaders whose job it was to safeguard the Islamic community, they claimed to be the inheritors of Muhammad's office who were infallible in both political and religious spheres.

Yet in another sense, the new style of Caliphate also saw a harkening back to the times of old, since it served to institutionalize tribal divisions, keeping power in the hands of the Quraysh family line, to which the Umayyad clan belonged. Although today in the twenty-first century there is no Caliph, the controversy over the succession and its powers continues to be debated. To this day there are those who believe that only a member of the Quraysh family line would make a legitimate Caliph, while others argue that the role should not be hereditary at all, but rather, in keeping with the Islamic spirit of equality, it should be open to every Muslim. For their part, the Hanafis (representing one of the four legal schools of Sunni Islam) maintained that the Caliphate had in fact lasted no more than thirty years and ended with Ali's death. From that point onwards, it held that there was only the government of kings, not Caliphs.

Once in power, the Umayyad successors saw their gains come in thick and fast. To the west, they oversaw the completion of the conquest of North Africa: Carthage in 698, and Tangier in 712. The conquests paved the way for the incorporation of Spain after a lightning assault on the Iberian Peninsula in the early years of the eighth century. Meanwhile, to the east the Umayyads extended Islamic rule beyond Persia, seizing territory in modern-day Pakistan and Central Asia. Balkh (in modern Afghanistan) had been conquered in 652, now they moved even further, taking Bukhara (in Uzbekistan) in 706-09, Taskhent (also in Uzbekistan) in 710, and Sind (in Pakistan) in 711. Added to this were

The Dome of the Rock and the Al-Aqsa Mosque

Sacred to Muslims, Jews, and Christians alike, the golden-roofed Dome of the Rock in Jerusalem was built during the reign of the Umayyads to commemorate Muhammad's Night Journey. In A.D. 620 he journeyed with the Archangel Gabriel to pray near the Rock with the other prophets and receive confirmation that he had chosen Islam, the one true religion.

For the Jews the Dome of the Rock is sacred because it stands on the Temple Mount, the site of Solomon's Temple, twice destroyed in ancient times and which the Jews believe must be rebuilt to herald the coming of the Jewish Messiah. Built atop the earlier location of the Temple, the Dome was constructed by the Umayyad ruler Abd al-Malik and completed in 691.

Located 200 meters to the south of the Dome is the Al-Aqsa Mosque. Umar, the Second Caliph, captured Jerusalem in 637 and, on entering the city, went up to the Temple Mount to pray. He publicly refused to pray where the Dome stands now, saying that if he did, then all Muslims would follow his example and build a mosque on top of the site that was holy to other religions too. Instead, he moved few meters away and prayed on his cloak—the spot where the Al-Aqsa Mosque was later built, thereby sealing Jerusalem's position as Islam's third most holy city after Mecca and Medina.

The original mosque was built in 715 but it has been destroyed numerous times by earthquakes. It has also attracted other no less turbulent events, seeing the assassination of King Abdullah of Jordan on its steps in 1951, and a fire caused by a deranged Australian tourist in 1969, which destroyed the beautiful 12th century wood and ivory pulpit. Meanwhile,

bullet holes in the walls of the Dome of the Rock bear witness to the bloody events of 1990, when militant Zionists attempted to enter the compound and place a cornerstone for the building of "a Jewish Third Temple." In the ensuing chaos Israeli trops killed more than 20 Palestinian protesters.

the former Persian territories in the Caucasus, which today make up Azerbaijan, Armenia, and Georgia.

The cornerstone of Umayyad fighting power was the army. However, with the Arabs far too small to make up the forces required to carry out such a huge campaign of conquest, the Umayyads were heavily dependent on non-Arab recruits who had converted to Islam, such as Turks and Berbers—the latter played a key role in the conquest of Spain. While the calvary was beginning to play an increasingly important role, it only would come to the fore under a successive dynasty, the Abbasids.

The navy also had a part to play at various points in history, yet it would generally prove to be of secondary interest—the Arabs, Berbers, Turks, and Persians had little by way of a naval tradition and tended to hold the sailors who sailed the Mediterranean Sea in low esteem. In their battles against the Byzantines, the Umayyads crewed their ships with the likes of Copts (Egyptian Christians), Greeks, and Syrians. One notable early Muslim victory at sea took place in 655, when the Arab navy destroyed the Byzantine fleet off the coast of modern Turkey in the Mediterranean at the Battle of the Masts.

In 750, the Umayyad dynasty came to an end after a rival faction, the Abbasids, who charged the rulers with corruption, staged a revolt and toppled the Caliph and his family in Damascus. The Caliph Marwan II attempted to flee but was hunted down and killed in the Egyptian town of Busiris. Eighty other leading Umayyads were butchered after being tricked into attending a banquet. Only one prince, Abd al-Rahman, managed to escape, and he would go on to found an independent Umayyad dynasty in Spain, thereby sowing the seeds of a great Islamic civilization in Europe itself.

Developments in Art and Architecture

Although immersed in their energetic pursuit of territorial gain, the Umayyads did find time to realize some artistic achievements, although most of what has survived is primarily related to architecture. Two of the greatest examples standing today are the Dome of the Rock at Jerusalem and the Great Mosque at Damascus.

Work on the Dome of the Rock was begun by Caliph Abd al-Malik in the middle of the 680s and completed in 691. Octagonal in plan and boasting a tall dome, this early example of Muslim architecture was principally influenced by Christian architecture of the Byzantine world, but also featured Persian Sassanian-influenced motifs.

The Great Mosque (built *c.* 705-14) at Damascus, which still survives in its more or less original form, also owes much to Byzantine architecture. Particularly striking features are the beautiful mosaics that adorn its walls and arcades. Wonderfully intricate, they feature abstract motifs, representations of villages, and vividly animated trees carpeted with green leaves, making them among the finest decorative mosaics to be found anywhere in the world.

One of the most notable aspects of Islamic art is the tendency to avoid representing human or animal forms. This resistance ultimately stems from the belief that the creation of living forms is unique to God, and as such, the role of images and image makers has been controversial. While the "Hadiths," or traditions of the Prophet's life, take a dim view of representational art, where painters of images are threatened with punishment on the Day of Judgment, in the Qur'an itself there is no clear ban. It does condemn idolatry and uses the Arabic term *musawwir* ("maker of forms," or "artist") as a specific epithet for God alone. It is a matter of great debate as to whether this attitude predates the ninth century, yet the absence of such art on the mosaics of the Dome of the Rock or the Mosque at Damascus suggests it may have.

The actual depiction of Muhammad and of other holy figures in Islam always has been discouraged. While some images of Muhammad did appear at certain periods, they continue to offend the sensibilities of most Muslims—in many cases their faces have been intentionally obscured, either by the artists themselves or at a later date. Nevertheless, in secular art, which thrived in Islamic societies, many artists gave full rein to their imaginations, depicting not only humans, but also conjuring up images of animals, monsters, and devils—often to spectacular effect.

Artists working in a religious context instead concentrated their efforts on less representational styles of art that were considered by the orthodox schools of thought to be more conducive to the contemplation of God. Religious art in general entered a fabulous, unparalleled period of abstract design. Throughout the Islamic world, Muslim artists produced exquisite geometrical designs in a variety of situations such as stone carvings, woodwork, and textiles.

A familiar artistic style used to great effect on the surfaces of mosques and buildings is that known as "arabesque," taken from the French, meaning "Arabic," which features intricate abstract geometrical and floral designs. In Islamic art it was a process often exploited to cover entire surfaces. The term is now applied to any complex, linear decoration based on flowing lines, including the Western European style that developed in Renaissance times.

Calligraphy also became a major feature of Islamic art, and throughout the centuries artists have devoted themselves not only to creating elaborate copies of the Qur'an but to adapting words and verses to the decorative arts. Arabic lettering varies from flowing cursive styles like Naskhi and Thuluth to the older, angular Kufic. On a traditional Islamic building, a number of different writing styles may appear on, for example, the walls, windows, or minarets. These inscriptions tend to be from the Qur'an and the Hadiths, and are in harmony with the religious purposes of the building.

Islamic Arabic calligraphy therefore represents divine power and beauty, not merely an art form but involving also divine and moral representations. Its history is the integration of artistry and scholarship. Through the abstract beauty of the lines, energy flows in between the letters and words, integrating the parts into a whole. The abstract beauty of Arabic calligraphy is not always easily comprehended—but this beauty will reveal itself to the discerning eye.

The Arabic Language—Instrument of Islam

Arabic is one of the world's major languages. Its unbroken literary tradition goes back more than thirteen centuries, and apart from being the language of Islam, it is also the written and spoken means of communication used across the entire breadth of North Africa, the Arabian Peninsula and the Middle East. The official language of eighteen nations alone, the total population of its speakers numbers around 120 million, placing it in the top ten tongues of the planet. The numerical, geographical, political, and cultural status of the language was formally recognized by the United Nations in 1973, when Arabic was made the sixth official language of that body along with English, French, Spanish, Russian, and Chinese.

Arabic belongs to the Semitic family of languages, which also includes Hebrew (both classical and modern), Aramaic, Syriac, and

Development of the Arabic Script

More revered than even the art of textiles in the Islamic world is calligraphy: the art of ornamental writing.

The Arabic script was developed expressly to write down the Qur'an, and Muslim scribes reproduced its words and verses in as beautiful a rendering as possible, adapted to a huge variety of surfaces, from architecture to the fragile pages of books. Perhaps it is only in China or Japan that calligraphy holds a similarly important position. As the ancient Arabic proverb says: "Purity of writing is purity of soul."

Numerous Arabic loanwords have filtered into European languages either directly from Arabic or via other, Islamized

ا	ā, '	ظ	ẓ
ب	b	ع	ʿ
ث	th	غ	gh
ج	j	ف	f
ح	ḥ	ق	q
خ	kh	ك	k
د	d	ل	l
ذ	dh, z	م	m
ر	r	ن	n
ز	z	ه	h
س	s	و	w, ū
ش	sh	ي	y, ī
ص	ṣ		
ض	ḍ	ء	ʾ
ط	ṭ	ة	a, at

Phonetic transcription of the Arabic alphabet

languages like Persian, Turkish and Swahili, particularly via science, the arts, and commerce. English is no exception and is filled with a wide range of loanwords that are common words today. Among these are:*

admiral—*amīrāl* (أميرال)
alchemy— *al-kīmīyā'* (الكيمياء)
alcohol—*al-kuḥūl* (الكحول)
algebra—*al-jibr* (الجبر)
alkali—*al-qily* (القلي)
arsenal—*al-ṣinā'a* (الصاعة)
assassin—*hashshashīn* (حشاشين)
coffee, cafe—*qahwa* (قهوة)
genie—*jinn* (جن)
guitar—*qitār* (قطار)
hazard—*khatar* (خطر)
lute—*al-'ūd* (العود)
magazine—*makhzan* (مخزن)

orange—*nāranj* (نارنج)
safari—*safar* (صفر)
saffron—*za'farān* (زعفران)
sandal—*sandal* (صندل)
sugar—*sukkār* (سكار)
syrup—*sharāb* (شراب)
tambourine— *tanbūr* (طنبور)
tariff—*ta'rifa* (تعرفة)
zero—*ṣifr* (صفر)

*Note that "al-" means "the" in Arabic.

42

Above are various forms of Islamic
script (top to bottom):
Simple Kufic—simple linear strokes.
Foliated Kufic—strokes are
embellished with leaf forms.
Floriated Kufic—foliated and rosette
embellishment is further increased.
Naskhi—a cursive form with some of
the Kufic foliation retained.
Thuluth—intensified cursive style.
Nastaliq—elegant form with the
placement of the elements executed
with almost careless ease.

several of the languages of Ethiopia (including Amharic). Its alphabet, with the occasional modification, is used to write other, non-Semitic languages as well, such as Persian, Kurdish, and Urdu (one of the official languages of Pakistan that is closely related to Hindi). Until the 1920s, Turkish also was written using a modified Arabic alphabet, as were several leading African languages, notably the West African language of Hausa and Swahili in East Africa. In the same way that Latin was used in Western Europe of old, Arabic was also commonly used throughout the spheres of Islamic influence as a literary language so that speakers of other languages could communicate on administrative, legal, scientific, and commercial matters.

The term "Arabic" itself is used to describe three different forms of the same language: Classical Arabic, which is the language of the Qur'an; Colloquial, or Spoken, Arabic, as used in the daily lives of the people of the Arab countries; and Modern Standard Arabic, sometimes also called Modern Literary Arabic.

The Qur'an was written down in Classical Arabic in its purest form about twelve centuries ago. It has always been a constant grammatical and linguistic authority affecting all Muslims and all speakers of Arabic regardless of their religion.

Colloquial Arabic shows great diversity from region to region and among different layers of the population. Moreover, the various dialects differ quite considerably from the written language in vocabulary and grammar, as well as syntax. Maltese, the language of the islands of Malta in the Mediterranean Sea, is the only form of Arabic that is written in the Roman script.

Modern Standard Arabic is the more formal language of newspapers, education, and broadcasting, and is common to all Arabic-speaking countries (with the exception of Malta). In many ways, it is quite close to Classical Arabic. Compared to Classical Arabic, Modern Standard Arabic is simpler in grammar and syntax, but the greater difference is in vocabulary.

The existence of a commonly accepted literary standard has therefore been a powerful unifying force in the written language. One of the results has been that today's Arabic as written in, say, a newspaper or a popular novel is much closer to the language of the Qur'an than modern Greek, for example, is to classical Greek, not to mention modern and medieval English, French, or German.

Non-Muslim Minorities in the Islamic World

The treatment of non-Muslim populations living under Islamic rule over the centuries is a complex subject and has been the source of a great deal of controversy. Yet, placed in context, especially when judged by medieval and later European standards, Islamic lands often provided an exceptional degree of tolerance. Such dealings were seldom arbitrary, but were usually underpinned by a system of law. The overall picture that emerges challenges the traditionally held European perception that Islam was an intolerant religion that was forced wholesale by the sword on subject populations.

Islam rules that "there is no compulsion in religion." Certainly a general lack of urgency to gain souls to Islam characterized the Arab conquests. Indeed, far from mirroring the rapid pace of Arab territorial expansion, conversion proved a slow process, and finding ways to accommodate large non-Muslim communities within the various Islamic states that emerged would turn out to be a challenging task, varying considerably according to local circumstances.

With regard to the Jews and Christians, there was an obligation for Muslims to respect them and endeavor to accommodate their communities within the Islamic state. Certainly, individual Muslim rulers often tailored the laws to suit their own needs, and incidents of religious persecution by Muslims are well documented. Nevertheless, forceful conversion was generally the exception and not the rule, and the deep-rooted institutional form of mass religious persecution so common in Christian European history by Catholics and Protestants alike has no real counterpart in the Muslim past.

The protection of the "People of the Book"—understood in Islam to mean Jews and Christians, on account of their belief in the Old Testament, and the Sabeans, who may have been Zoroastrians with their holy scripture the Avesta—had its roots firmly in the Qur'an, and, as such, under Islamic laws it was a duty for all Muslims to uphold their rights. Known as the "Protected People" (*Ahl al-Dhimma*) or *dhimmis*, the Jews, Christians, and Sabeans were to be allowed to practice their religion without hindrance or fear of persecution.

While every aspect of life for Muslims—be it birth, death, marriage, inheritance, property, or even the conduct of business—was encompassed by their own *Sharia* law, Christians and Jews living in the newly conquered lands mostly were left to apply their local laws according to their own customs and traditions. Communities chose their own leaders to act for them in their dealings with their Muslim overlords. There was a price to pay, however, and all able-bodied non-Muslim males were required to pay the Muslim authorities a special tax, known as *jizya*. They were also forbidden from bearing arms and as such were exempt from performing military service. They were not, however, required to pay *zakat*—the donation Muslims were obliged to make to charity.

The precedent for the treatment of non-Muslim subjects had been set during Muhammad's lifetime and during that of the first Caliphs. Despite Muslim hostility towards the Jews in Medina, Muhammad later set an example when, during an expedition to Tabuk (near the Gulf of Aqaba) in 630, he extended protection to both Jewish and Christian communities in exchange for a poll tax.

Abu Bakr, the First Caliph, also ordained that:

> If a province or people receive you, make an agreement with them and keep your promise. Let them be governed by their laws and established customs, and take tribute from them as is agreed between you. Leave them in their religion and their land!

The Caliph Umar was also credited with establishing a highly influential if harshly worded covenant between Muslims and non-Muslims. Certainly the *dhimmis* were subject populations, and the *jizya* tax and prohibition from carrying arms served to reinforce their subordinate relationship. Nevertheless, the onus was on the Islamic community to establish an arrangement with non-Muslims that amounted to a clear, constitutional contract, despite the fact that from time to time leaders or communities chose to ignore it.

Expansion of the Empire

As the Muslim realm expanded ever further, bringing an increasing diversity of cultures under its domain, new attitudes were encouraged that saw the arrangement extended to non-Christian or Jewish communities too. Accordingly, after the initial destruction that accompanied the conquests, in Persia and other former territories of the Sassanian Empire, the Zoroastrian populations were, for the most part, able to continue practicing their faith—once again on payment of the *jizya* tax. However, on occasion, zealous governors and officials broke treaties and harassed Zoroastrians and there were instances when their holy fire temples were destroyed.

In later centuries, India would prove especially challenging. There, Muslim rulers had to confront the practical challenges of controlling a vast non-Muslim population. After ferocious attacks on the Hindu population, their Muslim overlords had little choice but to eventually extend *dhimmi* status to the Hindus too, a decision that was helped somewhat by the knowledge that they had ancient religious scriptures of their own. Under the rule of the first Mughal emperors, Hindus and followers of other religions in India enjoyed a great deal of freedom.

Meanwhile, during the early period of conquest, the Arabs were in practice not overly concerned with the religious beliefs of their newly subjected populations. Nor did they have a clear intent to physically colonize their new dominions—it was only later, as the need for military conflict lessened, that more and more Arab Muslims began to be integrated into the social fabric of territories that lay outside the Arabian heartland.

The Arabs took care not to greatly interfere with the existing order in the land since it jeopardized the amount of wealth that could be extracted—a major concern given the expense of keeping their occupying armies satisfied. Having ensured that local rulers accepted their suzerainty, the Arabs merely allowed things to continue as they were. The payment of tribute was usually sufficient to ensure that local rulers were left to govern without too much interference. Governors, sent by the Caliph, generally limited themselves to the collection and payment of tribute and taxes and making sure the armies were paid. This arrangement logically discouraged any desires to convert the population since more Muslim converts meant less revenue, and more competition for privileges thus far reserved for the Arab overclasses.

Not infrequently, the Arabs found themselves as welcome invaders. Certainly, in the case of those peoples living on the peripheries of the great Sassanian and Byzantine empires, where imperially sponsored religious persecution was rife and high taxes were imposed, their lot was substantially improved by the arrival of the new Arab overlords.

In Egypt, for example, the Arabs came as something of a liberation force for the native Coptic Christian population—freeing them from

Jihad—the Struggle for Islam

The word "jihad" has been seen in the West as an indication of the aggressive stance of Muslims towards the non-Muslim world. In fact, this highly emotive word, literally meaning "struggle" or "great effort," is far more subtle and subject to various interpretations.

Some jurists considered it to be an obligation incumbent on Muslims to defend Islam by the sword, with results that were in practice more offensive than defensive. On the frontier lands, such as those dividing Muslim and Christian territories, as in Spain or Anatolia (Turkey), there were many willing recruits ready to die a martyr's death in the fight against the infidel—by becoming a martyr, or "shahid," the reward is immediate entry into Paradise. This interpretation has been used to great effect by modern Muslim political groups, such as Islamic Jihad, which are seen in the West as part of an ongoing historical religious war waged to force their version of Islam on the rest of the world, including on other Muslims.

Yet another entirely different interpretation is one that was nurtured by the Sufis, who became more preoccupied with winning the internal spiritual struggle of the self against the temptations of the world, a jihad that was necessary to gain knowledge of God. In a less mystical sense, jihad has been seen as an expression of the spiritual effort required to maintain one's faith in times of adversity, a true act of self defense.

Jihad as holy war against infidels and infidel countries is described in both the Holy Qur'an and in the Hadiths. With this in mind, Muslim law has divided the world into two entities: "Dar al-Islam" ("The World of Islam") and "Dar al-Harb" ("The World of War"). Battling against the "World of War" is a duty for a Muslim, as this is the only way for the peace of Islam to replace the warlike conditions of infidel society. These enemies of Islam are divided into two groups, the People of the Book (the "Ahl al-Kitab"), and pagans (the "Kafirun"). The first group, defined as Jews, Christians, and Zoroastrians, need only to submit to an Islamic ruler and live in peace with other Muslims to end the situation where jihad is imperative. For pagans there is a similar principle, but they are granted fewer rights. While this group generally can live safely within a Muslim society, some have ruled that they should either convert to Islam or face the death penalty. In situations where Muslim rulers order war to be waged against the infidels, they should be allowed sufficient time to convert before being attacked.

Jihad is a duty for every Muslim community, but not necessarily for every individual. It is sufficient that a certain number of able men perform jihad. While offensive jihad is fully permissible in Sunni Islam, it is prohibited for some of the larger Shi'i groups, who consider only their Imam, now in hiding, as having the right to decide whether to go to war or not. The third Islamic group, the Kharijis, whose uncompromising attitude killed the Caliph Ali, regard Jihad as an additional, sixth Pillar of Islam, a position that other groups of Islam have adhered to in the past.

Muslim thinkers and mystics often use the words "greater" and "lesser" to differentiate between the two concepts of jihad, with the former representing the struggle against the self and only the "lesser jihad" referring to warring in the path of God.

the heavy hand of the Byzantine authorities, under which they had languished for two centuries. Differing interpretations of Christianity had led to a concerted effort by the Byzantine authorities to forcefully impose religious uniformity in Christian Egypt. As a result, from 451 until the Arab conquests, Egyptian Christians, or Copts, were subjected to prohibitive taxes and ferocious treatment, including torture, supervised by the all-powerful Byzantine governor in Egypt. The Arabs were quick to grasp the situation and readily exploited it, offering the Copts preferential treatment and putting them in charge of the collection of *jizya* taxes levied on the rest of the non-Muslim population.

Status of Non-Muslim Subjects

Apart from taxes, a variety of other restrictions based on religious denomination were normally in force in the Islamic world, although these were seldom uniform but varied according to place and time.

For example, dress restrictions were commonly imposed on the *dhimmis*. Under the Caliph Al-Mutawakkil in 850, for instance, Christians were required to wear a yellow Persian mantle, a belt of cord, to fix two balls behind their saddles and to use wooden stirrups only. Hats were restricted to special colors, while turbans had to be yellow. It is also around this time that there is mention of the practice of obliging *dhimmis* to wear distinguishing colored patches that were sewn into their garments—a device that would crop up at various times in Islamic history. In the fourteenth century, the Mamluk dynasty that controlled Egypt and Syria imposed distinctive colors—yellow for Jews, blue for Christians, and red for Samaritans. In times when feelings against Christians ran especially high, it was not unknown for them to make life easier by borrowing items of clothing from the Jews.

Other restrictions related to places of worship, such as those preventing *dhimmis* from constructing churches, synagogues, or fire temples on new sites, and limiting them to repairing existing ones. Public displays of faith such as processions were looked down upon. Bells were liable to cause offense—Muhammad is believed to have declared disapprovingly, "The angels will not enter any house in which bells are rung." (Muslims are summoned to prayer by the call of a "muezzin," never by bells.)

Urfa (Edessa). During the Sassanian and Byzantine periods it was a major trade center—one of only two legal crossing points between east and west. According to tradition Urfa was the birthplace of the prophet Ibrahim (Abraham). The park behind the Mosque features the sacred Pool of Abraham filled with carp which believers down the centuries have fed.

In social relations, special rules also applied. While a Muslim man was permitted to marry a *dhimmi* woman, a *dhimmi* man was forbidden to marry a Muslim woman. *Dhimmis* often did certain jobs that Muslims rejected for religious or other reasons, yet this was seldom through coercion. As for most other jobs they were, technically, at least, not barred from taking them.

Dhimmis also usually enjoyed freedom of movement, although they tended to live in their own quarters in Muslim cities. Aside from a few exceptions these areas were not legally imposed by the authorities, and tended not to result in the isolated ghettos typical of Christian Europe.

At times, however, the *dhimmis* faced extremely tough conditions. The fanatical Almoravid and Almohad dynasties that ruled over Spain in the twelfth and thirteenth centuries, for example, broke with the overall tradition of tolerance in the land and persecuted non-Muslims. To the east, during the seventeenth century under the Indian Mughal Emperor Aurangzeb, the tolerant treatment extended to *dhimmis* by his ancestors was reversed. His heavy-handed approach led to widespread resentment and bloody rioting.

Often methods were employed not merely to distinguish religious minorities, but to intentionally segregate and oppress them. The fanatical Fatimid Caliph of Egypt, Al-Hakim, for example, used dress restrictions as part of a concerted campaign of persecution against Christians and Jews. He also, it appears, used this to bait his political rivals, the Abbasids—in 1004, he ordered non-Muslims to wear black turbans like those traditionally worn by the Abbasids, and later decreed that all their clothing should be black. Jews were also made to wear a block of wood carved to represent the Golden Calf of the Bible around their necks, while Jewish and Christian women were forced to wear shoes of mixed colors: one red and one black.

There were instances of ghettos, such as in Morocco and sometimes Persia. As late as the turn of the twentieth century, travelers in Shi'i Iran during the rule of the Qajar dynasty (which ended in 1925) reported on the abject conditions in which Jews continued to live. Confined to their ghettos, they suffered discriminatory and often degrading treatment from the Muslim population, and heavily restricted in terms of freedom of movement and employment opportunities. In certain

An ancient common Islamic symbol that is still common today, the fingers of the hand representing the Five Pillars of Islam.

documented cases, Jews even were prohibited from going in the streets during the rain lest the dirt from their bodies wash off and splash onto the feet of Muslims to contaminate them.

A report from 1907, paraphrased by the historian Bernard Lewis in *The Jews of Islam*, notes that in that same year a sheikh in the Persian province of Kermanshah, "with the support of the merchants and the artisans, issued sets of rules for both the Muslims and the Jews. The latter were required not to go out when it rained, always to wear the Jewish badge, not to build houses higher than those of Muslims, not to cut their side whiskers, and not to ride horses."

The Abbasids and
the Rise of Baghdad

*"The Abbasid rulers, with their more direct exposure to the Iranian idea of
an absolute king of kings, carried the evolution of the Caliphate to
absolutist monarchy further than any of their predecessors. The Abbasid
Caliphs lived in luxurious palaces, isolated from all but their most trusted
inner circle of courtiers and advisers. They came to identify themselves not
simply as successors to the Prophet but as 'shadows of God on earth,'
and they exercised vast powers over their subjects."*
—William L. Cleveland (A History of the Modern Middle East)

With the fall of the Umayyads at the hands of the Abbasids,
the center of Muslim power shifted from Damascus in
Syria to Baghdad, now in Iraq—a few miles from
Ctesiphon where the pre-Islamic Sassanian kings of Persia had ruled
their empire and which had been reduced to little more than a village.
From Baghdad, the Abbasids would oversee what is considered to be
the greatest age in the history of Islamic civilization. Exposed to the
strong cultural identity of the Persians—forged from an astonishingly
long history as a great empire—rich new layers would be added to the
colorful tapestry of Islamic culture

The Abbasids were a clan whose chief Abu al-Abbas al-Saffah
claimed descent from Muhammad's uncle Abbas. Abu al-Abbas
assumed the title of Caliph in 749, ruling under the title of
"Commander of the Faithful" or "Amir al-Mu'minin." It was his
brother and successor, Abu Ja'far, known as "The Victorious" or "Al-
Mansur," who oversaw the construction of the new Abbasid capital at
Baghdad. Dubbed the "City of Peace" (*Madinat al-Salam*) it
blossomed into one of the most spectacular cities history had seen,
and it attracted great wealth and culture from all around the known
world.

The capital, of which nothing original now survives, was
conveniently located on the fertile banks of the mighty River Tigris

and near to the River Euphrates, both vital links in the network of regional and international trade routes. It was reported that in choosing the site Al-Mansur had been counseled:

> It is best to settle here, midway between these four agricultural districts of Buq, Kalwadha, Qutrabbul, and Buduria. Thus you will have palm plantations on every side of you and water near at hand: if harvest fails or is late from one district, you can get relief from another. You can get provisions by the Sarat canal from the Euphrates river traffic: Egyptian and Syrian caravans will come here by the desert roads, and all kinds of China goods upriver from the sea, and Byzantine and Mosul produce down the Tigris. With rivers on both sides, no enemy can approach except by ship or bridge.

Baghdad was intended to be the very heart of the Muslim world. Built according to a circular plan, it was surrounded by high walls, towers and a deep moat—giving it the appearance of a fortress from the outside. It had four gates that opened towards Syria, the province of Khorasan, and the recently-founded Islamic cities of Basra and Kufa, in Lower Iraq. At the center was the imperial complex of the Dar al-Khilafa, featuring a splendid palace, about which little is known, and a large mosque. Above the Green Dome of the palace hall was a statue of a horseman that, according to tradition, would always point in the direction of the enemies of the Islamic empire. From early on the city was modified, and eventually swallowed up by surrounding urban development until its original form was lost. The Green Dome and horseman collapsed in the tenth century and the closest in spirit we can get to them is through images in a thirteenth-century manuscript depicting toys for a minor Turkish prince.

In physical terms, Baghdad reflected the absolute authority of the Caliphate over the Islamic world. Accordingly, an audience with the Caliph was never to be taken lightly. By the side of the throne stood the executioner with a strip of leather to catch the blood of the victim should the ruler order the summary execution of one of his subjects. Following in the style of the old Persian shahs, it was customary for those summoned before the court to kiss the ground before the Caliph, or, if more favored, to kiss his hand or foot.

The Golden Age

Under the Abbasids, the arts and sciences flourished as never before, unleashing an irrepressible intellectual energy that was destined to flow into the collective pool of knowledge that shaped the civilized world. The Caliph Harun al-Rashid (r. 786-809), the same ruler who later became the subject of many of the stories in the classic *Thousand and One Nights*, was a major patron of the arts. His leadership coincided with one of the greatest periods of the Caliphate, a time when diplomatic relations were maintained from France to China.

Under the patronage of Al-Mamun (r. 813-33), the famed House of Wisdom was built, and it became a center of research where scholars flocked to translate and interpret great works of other cultures into Arabic. Such efforts opened up a whole new world of ideas to Muslim thinkers, who pored over works such as those of Plato, Aristotle, and other great Greek Classics which they used in their own search to understand the world around them and their quest for spiritual truth. In so doing they preserved many of the great classical texts that were already lost in the West, and which would eventually be returned to Christian Europe in the centuries to come, primarily through the meetings of scholars in Muslim Spain. With a firm grounding in not only Greek but other Classics too, Muslim scholars also began to make their own unique contributions to the fields of medicine, arithmetic, geography, chemistry, and astronomy.

It is a fitting tribute to this period that the twentieth-century thinker Bertrand Russell wrote in his *History of Philosophy*: "Our use of the phrase 'The Dark Ages' to cover the period from 699 to 1000 marks our undue concentration on Western Europe." And indeed, while Europe languished in the near anarchy of petty kingdoms perpetually warring with each other, the Islamic world was rejoicing in its Golden Age of industry and enlightenment. The Islamic historian Bernard Lewis also noted: "Experimental science, Westerners like to persuade themselves, is peculiarly and exclusively Western. In fact, it was developed in medieval Islam much more than in the ancient world. The Greek genius lay in theory and philosophy. The Muslims developed experimental science and bequeathed a rich legacy which helped to start the modernization of the West."

Muslim scholars excelled in mathematics and it was through them that concepts such as the decimal system and Arabic numerals (the basis of those now used in the West) would gradually be introduced into Europe. Instrumental in paving the way for decimalization was the great mathematician Al-Khwarizmi (*c.* 780-850), whose work featured a point sign for zero. It was a concept that had made its way from India into Persia around the mid-eighth century after a number of imported Hindu works were translated into Arabic and subsequently modified.

Under the patronage of Al-Mamun, Al-Khwarizmi set the standard for future scholars, and the influence of his treatise, "The Compendious Book on Calculation by Completion and Balancing" (*Hisab al-Jabr wa 'l-Muqabala*) on the development of the subject cannot be underestimated. Translated into Latin during the twelfth century, it remained the principal mathematics textbook in European universities until the sixteenth century. (It is from *al-jabr* in Al-Khwarizmi's title that we get the word "algebra"; we also get the word "algorithm" from a corruption of his own name.)

An Unquenchable Thirst for Knowledge

It was not just in Baghdad that such a flowering of knowledge was taking place. The spirit of learning spread to other great cities of the Islamic world, from Spain to the borders of China, many of which came to rival and even surpass Baghdad. The key academic institutions in which the Islamic sciences were taught were the *madrasas*—teaching mosques, or religious colleges, primarily dedicated to training religious lawyers whose task it was to interpret Islamic Sharia law. During the tenth century, the prosperous city of Bukhara, which lay on the famed Silk Road, established a reputation as one of the major centers of theological and Islamic sciences, boasting a total of no less than a hundred *madrasas.*

Bukhara was also the birthplace of one of the greatest scientists of the medieval world, Ibn Sina, known to the West by his Latin name Avicenna (980-1037). Ibn Sina, who worked in a various courts, was a prolific writer in the fields of science, mathematics, theology, and philosophy and made important contributions to the study of contagious diseases, anatomy, and medicine. He had at his fingertips a wealth of literature that only could be envied in contemporary Europe.

Pioneers of Medicine

The Islamic world shone in the field of medicine. Having translated the Greek Classics on the subject, Muslim scholars began to make their own unique contribution, expounding new theories and developing treaments that are astonishingly modern in their approach. In Baghdad at its height there were numerous hospitals, some of which also included medical colleges and boasted libraries housing tens of thousands of books. Elsewhere in the Islamic world, where centers of learning and civilization had blossomed, other great hospitals were to be found, including in other great Islamic regions such as Egypt and Spain—the spectacular city of Cordoba alone was credited with more than fifty medical centers.

Medieval Muslim physicians routinely employed the practice of separating and isolating patients to avoid contagion. They developed sedatives and narcotic drugs to enable them to carry out operations, for which they invented hundreds of surgical instruments, employing animal intestines and silk to make sutures, and alcohol as an antiseptic. A particularly advanced operation was the removal of cataracts using a hollow needle and suction, a procedure that was only revived in 1846 in France. They also put forward advanced theories of blood circulation.

The five-volume "Medical Canon" of **Ibn Sina** (990-1037), containing more than a million words, offered a comprehensive overview of the body of medical knowledge known at the time. Translated into many languages, it became a standard work of reference in European medical schools until the seventeenth century. **Al-Arazi** (Razes) (841-926), also a much-translated author, wrote a treatise on measles and smallpox that clearly identified the difference between the two diseases, a work that still is valid to this day. **Al-Zahrawi** (Albucasis) (936-1013) was a Muslim Spanish surgeon *par excellence*. He described and performed numerous complex operations and also designed surgical instruments. Among the procedures that figure in his works are tracheotomies, the stripping of varicose veins, cauterization and ligatures to prevent bleeding, and numerous others relating to ear, cranial, and dental problems. He was also the first physician to provide a clear written description of hemophilia, recognizing the hereditary nature of the disease.

Ibn Sina (right) shown with the Greek thinkers Hippocrates and Galen in a medieval depiction of the three great masters of medical science.

For example, the Sultan of Bukhara's library boasted rooms of chests packed with books cataloged according to a range of subjects such as theology, law, logic, medicine, or poetry.

Writing almost exclusively in Arabic, Ibn Sina produced numerous works including commentaries on the works of Aristotle, and two great encyclopedias: "Healing" (*Al-Shifa*) and "Delivery" (*Al-Naja*). Yet it is for his "Laws of Medicine" or "Canon" (*Al-Qanun fi 'l-Tibb*), an in-depth survey of medical knowledge stretching from ancient to contemporary times, that he will be most remembered. The work eventually found its way into Europe where it was translated into Latin as early as the twelfth century and became a standard medical textbook that was in use up until the seventeenth century. Such was the academic importance of Arabic texts in mathematics, medicine, chemistry, and astronomy, that in the ancient English universities of Oxford and Cambridge mastery of the language became highly rated.

The unquenchable thirst for knowledge saw Muslim scholars casting their nets ever further, an example of which is the great scholar and scientist Al-Biruni (973-1048), a contemporary of Ibn Sina, who traveled extensively in India. Born in Khiva (in modern Uzbekistan), he was employed in the court of Sultan Mahmud of Ghazna, who ruled over an independent Muslim kingdom that had emerged in the region of Afghanistan.

During his stay in India Al-Biruni learned the fundamentals of Hindu philosophy, geography, and mathematics, repaying his teachers in turn by instructing them in Greek and Arabic philosophy and science. The scientist famously set down his observations of the Indian Subcontinent in "The Book of India" (*Kitab al-Hind*), an insightful work that details social and historical conditions in the region. The breadth of his studies later enabled him to bring together Arab, Greek, and Hindu theories on medicine and mathematics.

The Caliphate Weakens

Despite the continuation of the great cultural achievements and the spread of Islam, Abbasid political power began to decline from the mid-ninth century onwards. Already, by the earlier part of the century the dramatic phase of Arab expansion had ground to a halt.

With such a huge empire, it was a near-impossible task for the

Caliphs in Baghdad to keep a tight rein on their provincial governors or the countless local strongmen who were ready to flex their political muscle given the slightest opportunity. In fact, some gained sufficient power to enable them to establish their own dynasties, although often they took the precaution of nominally declaring their allegiance to Baghdad.

In Egypt, for example, the governor Ibn Tulun acquired a formidable range of political and military powers and effectively ruled as an independent leader from 868, despite professing to recognize Abbasid suzerainty. He built up a huge army of as many as 100,000 men, a large number of whom were slaves, and he even managed to extend his influence northwards into a good part of Syria.

Rather than channelling wealth out of Egypt and into the imperial coffers of Baghdad, Ibn Tulun held on to the taxes he raised and plowed much of the proceeds into a booming program of public works. It was a period that saw the creation of some of the finest architecture in Egypt. The baked-brick Mosque of Ibn Tulun, which still stands in Cairo, is famous throughout the world and features the oldest prayer tower or "minaret" in the country.

Ibn Tulun wielded such power that he even was able to establish his own dynasty in Egypt, although it was a short-lived affair. Once the strong hand of the founder was no longer on the reins of power, his successors soon lost their own grip on the country. The end came in 905, when the Abbasids stepped in once more and imposed a new governor who was answerable to the Caliph in Baghdad, although their problems with the rogue state were far from over.

The Abbasid Caliphate suffered a major blow in 945 from which it would never recover. With its leadership riven by interfactional fighting, a tribal group from the eastern Abbasid Empire, the Buyids, seized their moment and marched unchallenged into Baghdad, taking over the reins of power in Persia and Iraq. Although recent converts to Shi'i Islam—the cause that recognized Muhammd's son-in-law Ali and his successors as the legitimate leaders of the Muslim world—the Buyids in reality took little interest in religious affairs. Nor were they much interested in the governing of the state, preferring to pursue their own agenda of increasing their personal wealth from their newly gained territories.

To the west, there were more worries in store for the beleaguered Abbasids. As we shall see, two very different major rival states, the

The Mosque of Ibn Tulun—built in 879 it features an early example of a minaret, an architectural feature which first appeared in the seventh century. Muhammad declared that the call to prayer five times a day should be from the highest rooftop nearest to the mosque and, in time, minarets became an integral part of the actual mosque itself.

Fatimids of Egypt and a branch of the Umayyads in Spain, swiftly rose to prominence in the tenth century, stealing the limelight from Baghdad. Significantly, the leaders of both states would also style themselves Caliphs and both would make their own unique contribution to the Islamic world.

While dreams of building a coherent centralized worldwide Muslim state now began to look less likely amidst the political fragmentation that was taking place, Islam itself was, nevertheless, flourishing as never before, nurtured by the extensive trade routes of the Islamic world that tied a diversity of peoples in a common pursuit. Through trade routes, the religion coursed into new regions, making its way further southwards into Africa and eastwards into India and eventually into Southeast Asia and the edges of the Pacific Ocean.

As for the Abbasids, they still had an important part to play, long after the wane of their empire. The family would continue to produce a succession of Caliphs, fulfilling, for Sunni Muslims at least, the strong need for a temporal figurehead in the Muslim world.

Turkfication under the Seljuks

With the Abbasid Caliphate in crisis, overrun by the Shi'i Buyids, it would take the efforts of a Turkic-speaking people, the Seljuks, to revive Baghdad's fortunes. The Seljuks were descendants of the nomadic Oguz Turkic tribes that lived in Central Asia and part of present-day southeast Russia. Recent converts to Sunni Islam, they took their name from Seljuk, a prominent tenth-century leader of their people.

Pattern on a Seljuk tile from Anatolia, eleventh century.

Driven by overpopulation of the dry plains of their ancestral homelands, the warlike nomads had moved south and westwards under Seljuk's grandson Togrul Beg. In 1040, they entered Khorasan, a region lying in the northeast of Persia, where they settled for a while. Then, boosted by the support of the Abbasids who wished to topple their unwelcome Shi'i guests, the Seljuks seized the initiative and marched effortlessly into Baghdad in 1055. Togrul Bey was subsequently proclaimed Sultan.

With the fervor of new converts, the Seljuks took it on themselves to champion the Sunni cause, rallying Muslims under the banner of their Caliphate at Baghdad. Careful to retain political power for themselves as sultans, they maintained the Abbasid line of Caliphs as figureheads and symbols of religious unity.

The Persian historian Anne K. Lambton describes this innovative power-sharing arrangement as follows:

> Patriotism was an unknown virtue. All the Sultan expected of his subjects was that they should pay their taxes and pray for his welfare, while they expected from him security and justice. The state did not demand, or receive, the loyalty of the common man. Loyalty, so far as it transcended the bounds of the tribe, guild, quarter, or city, was accorded not to the state but to Islam.

In the 1060s, Togrul Bey's successor Alp Arslan consolidated the Seljuks' hold over Persia and extended their rule into neighboring territories. An important development in Islamic history was the extension of Seljuk control into the Christian lands of the Byzantine Empire and the creation of the separate Seljuk empire known as the Sultanate of Rum. The name Rum originated from the Arabs, who referred to the geographical entity of Anatolia, today occupied by Turkey, as *Bilad al-Rum*. It means roughly "land of the Romans," in recognition of the region's attachment to the Byzantine Empire. The Seljuks eventually overran much of the region between 1071 and 1081.

Persia Flourishes Again

After years of economic turmoil and regional instability the new Seljuk government in Baghdad breathed a new lease of life into Persia, bringing new security to the trade routes of the region—the traditional source of Persian wealth—and in the process facilitating the further spread of Islam.

This period of economic prosperity produced a boom in the arts. Most notable is the rich tradition of pottery of the period that demonstrates a mastery of complex techniques, featuring colors and intricate decorations in the form of living creatures such as birds, fish, horses, and humans. The Seljuk sultans also proved to be great patrons of architecture, they left a legacy of wonderful mosques, including the spectacularly beautiful Masjid-e Jami at Esfahan (completed in 1088).

Paradoxically, for a period initiated by nomadic illiterate barbarians such as the Seljuks, the era proved to be an unlikely but much-needed renaissance. With no literary tradition of their own, the Seljuks adopted Persian as their written language, promoting its use across their empire for affairs of state and popular literature. Sidelined to a certain degree, Arabic nonetheless retained its pre-eminence, and was used principally for Qur'anic and other religious studies.

Between the eleventh and thirteenth centuries, the numerous northwestern principalities of the Caucasus similarly experienced a cultural explosion which saw Persian literature flourish, bringing to light the highly influential poet—Nizami Ganjavi.

Nizami (born *c.* 1145) hailed from Ganja, now in the Republic of Azerbaijan, where he lived and worked all of his life. His genius for

The Sharia

The Sharia is an all-embracing system of Islamic law that is intended to inform a person's life from the cradle to the grave. More than simply sanctioning punishments and dispensing justice, it offers guidance in the totality of religious, poitical, social, domestic and private life. It is also held by Muslims that the full realization of the Sharia would give rise to the ideal state, one in which ultimately no line is drawn between religion, society, or politics.

The Sharia can be divided into two mains areas of regulations: those concerning worship and ritual duties; and those of a juridical and political nature. Except in those countries that have gone through a phase of Islamization (for example Sudan, Iran, and Saudi Arabia) many parts of the Sharia are not put into practice in Muslim societies. Nevertheless, the Sharia still holds great importance in domestic judicial fields such as family, marriage, and inheritance.

In an attempt to ascertain the legal principles of Islam, in the early centuries scholars developed a set of hierarchical procedures. The primary source was the Qur'an, the ultimate reference by which all Muslim lives are led. A second source of guidance and clarification was the Hadiths, the sayings and actions of Muhammad, which were consided exemplary. Great pains were taken to ensure the veracity of the Hadiths. For an incident to be accepted as authentic it was necessary to establish an unbroken chain of witnessess leading all the way to a Companion of the Prophet who witnessed it personally. While there are several major collections, those compiled by Al-Bukhari (810–70) and Muslim (819-875) are considered to be the most reliable commentaries and second in authority only to the Qur'an.

While numerous schools (*madhdabs*) of jursiprudence emerged throughout history, within the orthodox Sunni tradition there are four which are dominant in particular regions. These emerged during the eighth and ninth centuries, and each took its name from its founding jurist: Malik (*d.* 795; dominant in North and West Africa); Hanafi (Central Asia); Shafi (Egypt, East Africa, and the Far East); and Hanbali (Saudi Arabia).

Despite their own particular approaches to the law, they are, nevertheless, in agreement over the imporant issues and, through *fiqh* (the science of Sharia) their most respected scholars will issue *fatwas* or legal opinions or edicts as circumstances demand. While over the course of the centuries the schools came to be viewed as standard, none of these jurists ever claimed to be divinely inspired.

Traces of many non-Muslim juridical systems of non-Muslim origin can be seen in areas of the Sharia, such as Old Arab Bedouin law, commercial law from Mecca, agrarian law from Medina, law from the conquered countries, Roman law, and Jewish law. The Shi'is also have their own law schools, the most dominant of which is known as the Jafari school of law.

verse radiated outwards from the lofty mountains of the Caucasus across the Persian-speaking world, earning him an enduring reputation as a literary giant in the language. His "Treasury of Secrets" (*Makhzan al-Asrar*), an enigmatic philosophical poem, so profoundly impressed the ruler of the northern Caucasian city of Derbend, a port on the Caspian Sea, that he made a gift of a Qipchaq slave girl, named Afaq, whom the writer married and with whom he had a son. Her death inspired the grieving poet to write one of the greatest pieces of Persian literature, the intensely moving love poem entitled "Khusrow and Shirin." Nizami's popularity never waned and his works, which also included the love epic "Layla and Majnun," later became a popular subject for illustrated Persian manuscripts in the fifteenth and sixteenth centuries.

The Fatimids—Shi'i Rivals to Baghdad

Since the civil war that had erupted between Muslims over the leadership of the Islamic community, the Shi'is, had begun to gain a great deal of influence in certain key regions. As we have seen, the wily Buyids had managed, albeit temporarily, to become the temporary overlords of the Abbasid Caliphs in Baghdad. Yet, during the latter part of the tenth century, a new and far more enduring dynasty, the Fatimids, emerged as a major new power in the Middle East. The Fatimids, who hailed from Tunisia and dominated northwestern Africa, claimed to be descendants of Fatima, Muhammad's daughter and Ali's wife. Taking advantage of the situation in Egypt, which had been severely weakened by political upheavals, they launched an invasion in 969, encountering little resistance.

That same year, Cairo (from the Arabic "Al-Qahira" meaning "The Victorious,") became the new Fatimid capital. Extending their control further into Palestine and Syria, the Fatimids would soon be in a position to flaunt their power in front of their steadily weakening rivals in Baghdad, boosting the standing of their territories and injecting new vigor into regional trade.

The Shi'i dynasty brought Egypt a degree of independence it had not enjoyed since the days of the great Pharaohs. Furthermore, it put Egypt squarely on the map as a major cultural and spiritual center of the Muslim world, a reputation which it continues to enjoy to this day.

Islamic Art and Architecture

In contrast to Western art, in which painting and sculpture are dominant, it is in the so-called decorative arts that Islamic art found its primary means of expression. For the first time in history, the Islamic Empire linked together such varied and distant peoples as Spaniards, Africans, Persians, Turks, Egyptians, and Indians. Through this diversity an immediate spread of knowledge and blend of artistry arose. Three major periods are generally recognized: the Formative Period (650-1000), Middle Period (1000-1250), and Late Period (1250 on).

From its inception Islamic art was an art created for the setting of daily life. Most religious architecture, notably the mosque and the minaret, was built less as a testimonial to God than as a place where people could best express their piety and learn the precepts of the faith. In addition to forms used to decorate buildings, Islamic painting developed primarily in the shape of book illustration and illumination. Such painted works generally were created not as ends in themselves but to help explain a scientific text or to enhance the pleasure of reading history or literature.

Various ewer motifs from tiles in Tawrizi, Damascus, and Cairo.

In the field of the decorative arts the Islamic style is distinguished by the extraordinary techniques used in the making of utilitarian objects. These include the application of glazes and rich colors in ceramics and glassware; intricate silver inlays on bronze metalwork, lavish molded stucco and carved wood wall panels, and endlessly varied motifs woven into textiles and rugs. From Cordoba in Spain to Samarkand in Central Asia, the great cities of Islam were the centers of learning and of mercantile wealth. Of the thousands of ceramic objects excavated in the Persian city of Nishapur, the celebrated lusterwares from Fatimid Cairo, or the many inlaid bronzes from Herat (Afghanistan) or Mosul (Iraq), most were made for the bourgeoisie of the cities. In addition to the arts created for the urban

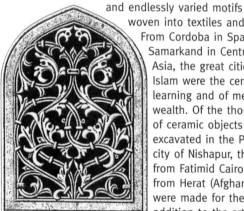

Animal motif on a twelfth-century Persian dish.

strata of the Islamic world, there was a splendid art of kings and emperors, exemplified by the countless treasures in the Topkapi Palace in Istanbul, built by the Turkish Ottomans.

A fundamental characteristic of much of Islamic art is its powerfully decorative ornamental quality. Calligraphic, geometric, and floral designs—such as the swirling, interlaced arabesque—were especially favored when creating motifs taken from nature or from an idealized version of the natural world.

Among the most prestigious and highly valued objects of all were textiles, which, in the Islamic world, served more than purely utilitarian or decorative purposes. Sometimes produced by imperial factories, they were used not only in homes, palaces, and mosques, but also served as gifts, rewards, and signs of political favor. The Muslim weavers adopted and developed the textile traditions of Sassanian Iran and the Mediterranean region (the latter were best known through Coptic textiles from Egypt).

The art of carpet-making was developed to a particularly high degree in Iran and Anatolia where the need for protection against the winter cold made the carpets indispensable

Velvet cushion cover with central eight-pointed star bordered with star-shaped flowers and tulips, eighteenth-century Turkey.

both in the shepherd's tent and in the prince's palace. In houses and palaces built of stone, brick, plaster, and glazed tile, carpets also provided a contrasting texture as floor and divan coverings and wall hangings.

One of Egypt's most famous landmarks is the Al-Azhar Mosque in Cairo. It was founded by the Fatimids in the tenth century and, ever since, it has remained a source of immense pride for Muslims. Its prestigious teaching institution is considered to be the oldest university in existence and continues to attract scholars from around the world. Al-Azhar was originally intended to train preachers to propagate Shi'i ideas, but under the rule of the great Muslim hero, Saladin, in the twelfth century it became a Sunni university. It was here that certain traditions seen in European universities were originated, including the wearing of black academic gowns, and the division of undergraduate and graduate faculties.

Egypt Flourishes under the Fatimids

From Cairo, the Fatimids pursued a policy of expansion into territories beyond the Egyptian frontiers, boasting governors in eastern Libya, western Saudi Arabia, and as far north as Damascus in Syria. Furthermore, they commanded the allegiance of local rulers from several other Mediterranean lands.

The Fatimids justified their political strength through the outright rejection of the legitimacy of the Abbasid Caliphate in Baghdad. Their style of leadership was deliberately steeped in the Shi'i tradition, resulting in a succession of Fatimid Caliphs upon whom rested absolute political and religious authority combined. Their supporters believed them to be divinely guided figures destined to impose Islamic justice throughout the world.

At first, the Fatimid Caliphs and their followers made a great deal of trouble for their rivals in Baghdad, bullying and cajoling them and sending missionaries to preach their own brand of Islam to the Abbasid population. In 1058, the Abbasids were even forced to suffer the indignity of acknowledging Fatimid supremacy.

Despite their zealous foreign policy, at home in Egypt the Fatimids proved considerably more relaxed—especially after they had consolidated their leadership. Life for the majority of the population continued much as it had before. Indeed, Shi'ism as a doctrine primarily was restricted to the elite and never adopted by the population at large.

During the early period of Fatimid rule, Egypt flourished economically and culturally. The pinnacle of their rule coincided with the enlightened reign of Caliph Abu-Mansur Nizar al-Aziz, from 975 to 996. It was a period that saw a boom in the construction of palaces, mosques, bridges, and canals in and around Cairo, making the city a true world capital.

The Fatimid dynasty also became a vital player in international trade, facilitating trade between destinations as far apart as India and Spain, as well as maintaining relations with Byzantium and promoting commerce with the wealthy Italian city-states. The connection with these European partners in trade was, nevertheless, an uneasy one since it was the Fatimids who had built the only substantial navy of the period. As great patrons of science and learning, the Fatimid Caliphs encouraged a great deal of research into astronomy and geography, two fields that put the empire in good stead as a naval power. Their fleets were the scourge of the western Mediterranean— even before seizing power in Egypt they already had taken Malta, Sardinia, Corsica, the Balearics, and, for a time, Genoa.

Apart from the thriving commercial empire he helped create, Caliph Nizar al-Aziz was also noted for the tolerance he extended to his Christian and Jewish subjects. However, his successor Al-Hakim, the sixth Fatimid Caliph (r. 996-1021), proved less tolerant than his predecessor, and exhibited fanatical tendencies. Not only did he persecute Christians and Jews living in Fatimid territories, he also targeted other sections of the population with a whole array of prohibitions that forbade, among other things, keeping dogs or playing chess. Shoemakers were forbidden to make women's shoes, and any woman unfortunate enough to be caught going to the public baths faced the alarming prospect of being bricked up alive in the building itself. It was Al-Hakim, whose mother was a Christian, who ordered the destruction in 1010 of one of Christendom's most holy shrines, the Church of the Holy Sepulcher in Jerusalem. The act, the exact reasons for which remain something of a mystery, helped to justify the future invasion of the Middle East and the Holy Land by the Christian Crusaders.

As Caliph Al-Hakim became ever more extreme and brutal in his policies, he became increasingly unpopular. He took frequent strolls through the streets of Cairo accompanied by a burly slave named Mas'ud who cruelly punished cityfolk who had committed minor crimes. Al-Hakim's slave made enough of an impression to enter the city's rich folklore in the expression "Stop it, or I'll call Mas'ud!"— used light-heartedly by people who are irritated.

Eventually, the Caliph's position became untenable. One night, while out on a donkey ride, he simply disappeared, never to be seen again—most probably murdered by his own family. However, he was not forgotten. A religious sect known as the Druzes, who held Al-Hakim to be divine, maintained that he had actually gone into hiding and would make his grand reappearance to usher in the Millennium. The sect continues to this day with communities in Syria, Israel, and Jordan, and, especially, Lebanon. Its scriptures are shrouded in secrecy, guarded by a select few and withheld from the rest of the faithful.

As the years went by, the Fatimid regime began to slide inexorably into an abyss of sustained crises and factional fighting. Abroad, the Fatimids began to lose control over their territories, and at home, real power was being usurped by powerful "viziers," or "chief ministers," who ruled in place of inexperienced and ineffectual young Caliphs.

Stylized image of a horseman used to decorate a tenth-century plate, Iraq.

Before long, the country was plunged into one of its darkest periods. Caliphs, viziers, and military cliques all vied for the throne, as if engaged in a bizarre and macabre form of musical chairs. Court intrigues, plots, and murder became the order of the day, as the country struggled under ever-increasing taxation.

The end arrived mercifully in 1171, at the hands of one of the Islamic world's greatest leaders, Saladin, who, as we shall see, was instrumental in restoring Sunnism to the country.

Al-Andalus
—Islam in Spain

"I do not understand how something
which lasted eight centuries can
be called a 'reconquest.' "
—José Ortega y Gasset, Spanish writer and thinker

Over the course of the centuries following the Umayyad invasion of 711, until the fall of the last Muslim kingdom of Granada in 1492, Islam would become an integral part of the political and social landscape of Spain. Moreover, "Al-Andalus," as Spain was known in Arabic (and the origin of the word "Andalucía," by which Southern Spain is known today), would become a colorful interface between the Islamic and Christian worlds. Its great centers of learning were beacons of civilization in the western Muslim world that shone a light far into Europe of the Dark Ages and helped to illuminate its path towards the Renaissance.

Prior to its conquest by the Arabs, the Iberian Peninsula, once a thriving province of the Roman Empire known as Hispania, had spent two centuries in steady decline under the rule of the Visigoths. Descendants of the warlike Goths from Germanic Northern Europe, the Visigoths had exploited their position as mercenaries for the rapidly disintegrating Roman Empire and seized Spain for themselves. They subsequently made Toledo their capital and in time established Catholicism as the official state religion. However, by the time of the crowning of the last Visigoth king, Rodrigo, in 710, the kingdom was barely under control, plagued by civil war and rebellious mountain tribes in the north of the country.

From the shores of what is today Morocco, the Muslims could see the coast of southern Spain shimmering tantalizingly over the dangerous and unpredictable strait between the Atlantic Ocean and the Mediterranean Sea that separates the African Continent and Europe—no more than nine miles at its narrowest point. Heading the expedition was the great general Tariq, who landed a Berber army by the huge majestic rock that was dubbed *Jabal Tariq* meaning "Tariq's Rock" in Arabic, from which present-day Gibraltar gets its name, a testimony to the momentous event that heralded a new Muslim order in Spain.

Heading westwards along the coast, his army confronted King Rodrigo and his men at the Battle of Guadalete, not far from the port of Cádiz, in July 711. The Visigoths, reflecting the disarray of the country as a whole, presented a far from united front and were soundly defeated. Rodrigo himself disappeared without a trace, most likely killed in the fighting.

The Muslims marched northwards towards the center of Spain encountering little resistance before finally reaching the Visigoth capital of Toledo. Backed by reinforcements led by the governor of North Africa, Musa ibn Nasayr, they soon took the city.

By 714, practically the entire Iberian Peninsula lay under control of the Muslim armies who now turned their sights on France. Pushing past the Pyrenees (the mountain range that forms a natural barrier separating Spain from the rest of Europe), they took the southern French city of Narbonne in 719. Continuing northwards to within 200 miles of Paris, they reached the Loire Valley, where, having overstretched themselves and become weakened in resources and supplies, they were defeated by the Frankish ruler Charles Martel at the Battle of Poitiers in 732.

The battle has been hailed by some historians as a decisive moment, one that prevented the Muslims from completely overrunning Europe. The famous eighteenth-century historian and thinker Edward Gibbon declared that had the Arabs not been defeated, "the Arabian fleet might have sailed without a combat" across to England into the mouth of the River Thames, further adding that "perhaps the interpretation of the Qur'an would now be taught in the schools of Oxford."

Other historians, however, remain skeptical, maintaining the importance of the battle to have been exaggerated, when in reality it was little more than a skirmish. Whatever the case, the fact that the Muslims were able to launch an attack so far into France is an indication of how well established they already were in Europe and how unstable the historic frontiers were between the Islamic and Christian European worlds.

Europe meets Africa—the Rock of Gibraltar where Tariq landed his troops in 711. The land mass in the background is Morocco, a distance of only a few miles. Gibraltar and Mt. Acha, which lies across the Straits, were known in Classical times as the Pillars of Hercules.

The Umayyads of Spain

While the Muslims had little difficulty toppling the Visigoths, keeping order in the newly conquered land of Al-Andalus proved an immensely challenging task for the Umayyad Caliphate, attempting to remotely control their newly acquired lands from their far-off capital of Damascus. In fact, the main source of trouble came from the Muslim forces of occupation—the boundless energy of the Arab and Berber armies in Spain was matched by their fiercely independent streak, which bordered on the anarchic.

Further uncertainty was to come with the unseating of the Umayyads by the Abbasid dynasty in 750. Yet, in a surprise move, it was to Spain that a surviving "emir" (prince) of the Umayyads, Abd al-Rahman, fled after the massacre of his family by the Abbasids. There he took the title of Emir of Al-Andalus, allowing the fallen dynasty a remarkable new lease on life there for many years to come.

Despite the ongoing dramas and conflicts in the peninsula, the early Spanish Umayyads managed to find enough breathing space to lay the foundations of the magnificence that was to follow. Already, by 785,

71

work had begun on the great mosque at their capital in Cordoba. While the ninth century saw Cordoba increase in standing in terms of cultural and artistic developments, it was the Emir Abd al-Rahman III who finally managed to impose firm central rule, thereby creating the conditions for Muslim Spain to fully blossom.

Coming to the throne in 912, he brought an end to the rebellions and internal disorder that had continued to plague the kingdom as a result of the fractious nature of the Arabs and Berbers. In 926, he dared to assume the all-powerful role of Caliph, and under his own rule and that of his three successors, the Islamic Caliphate of Cordoba reigned supreme in the Iberian Peninsula. The precarious Christian territories in the north of the peninsula had little choice but to bow to Cordoba's will and pay tribute.

The city of Cordoba that Abd al-Rahman III and his successors ruled over was truly spectacular. At its peak, with a population that may have reached as many as 100,000, it was the largest, the wealthiest, and the most civilized city in Western Europe. It had large markets, clean well-lit paved streets, running water, baths, mosques, and as many as fifty hospitals—all a far cry from the dark, filthy, and disease-ridden cities to be found in the rest of Europe.

The city gained an outstanding reputation for learning and scholarship. The study of the arts and sciences flourished and included astronomy, medicine, and mathematics. Under the patronage of the Caliphs, especially during the reign of Al-Hakim II between 961 and 976, Cordoba boasted one of the greatest libraries in the Islamic world and one without rival in Europe. In fact, its reputation was such that it attracted not only scholars from the Islamic and Arab world but also Christians from around Europe. The city also had a thriving Jewish population, and Cordoba became a major center for Hebrew scholarship.

New industries also thrived in Muslim Cordoba, which boasted glassware and pottery of exceptional quality. Similarly, highly skilled silk weavers and carpet makers ensured that their excellent products became famed throughout the Iberian Peninsula.

Spain—A Melting Pot of Cultures

While much of the population in Al-Andalus did convert to Islam, a substantial minority retained their faith. As in other parts of the

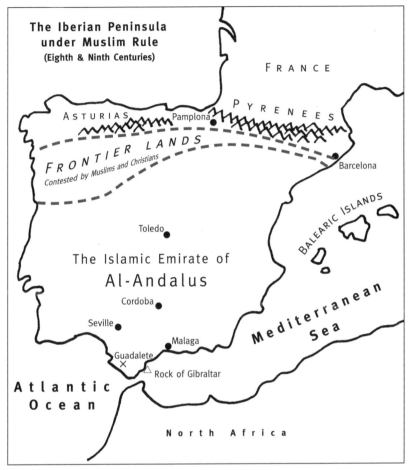

Muslim world, non-Muslims were still expected to pay the *jizya* tax, for which they could expect the protection of the state. Accordingly, churches and synagogues continued to function, with priests and rabbis going about their business administering to the needs of their congregations—although conspicuously public displays of faith, such as bells and processions, were discouraged. Some Christians even held positions of authority at the court of Cordoba.

The Christians living in Muslim Spain came to be known as "Mozárabes," a term that reflected their gradual isolation from the Christians of Western Europe and fostering of certain Arabic traits, such as dress, and their adoption of the Arabic language. The term

Mozárabe is the Spanish corruption of the Arabic *Musta'rib*, meaning to assimilate to Arab ways. The ancient church liturgy in Arabic used by the Christians of Toledo is commonly known as *Mozarabic*.

In 854, the Christian writer Alvaro lamented the laxity of those of his own faith:

> My fellow Christians love to read the poems and romances of the Arabs; they study the Arab theologians and philosophers, not to refute them, but to form a correct and elegant Arabic. Where is the layman who now reads the Latin commentaries on the Holy Scriptures, or who studies the

Ibn Rushd (Averroes) (1126-1198). The Cordoban-born thinker whose works had a profound influence on both Muslim and Christian thought.

> Gospels, prophets, or Apostles? Alas! All talented young Christians read and study with enthusiasm the Arab books; they gather immense libraries at great expense; they despise the Christian literature as unworthy of attention. They have forgotten their language. For every one who can write a letter in Latin to a friend, there are a thousand who can express themselves in Arabic with elegance, and write better poems in this language than the Arabs themselves.

It was not only the Christians who were thriving. The arrival of the Muslims had come as a great relief to the Spanish Jews. Under the Visigoths, Spanish Jews had been subjected to vicious campaigns forcing them to convert to Christianity or face punitive taxes, the confiscation of their possessions, or even slavery. Accordingly, many Jews who had fled Spain to escape hardship under the Visigoths took advantage of the new laws and returned to Spain. Under the Muslims, their life greatly improved and their own culture began to flourish.

With Muslims, Jews, and Christians all living side by side, customs and traditions overlapped, and Spain became a veritable melting pot. Furthermore, in time, intermarriages between Berbers, Arabs, and

Europeans caused physical characteristics to become similarly intermingled throughout the peninsula. The diverse mixture of Muslim peoples who made their way to Spain should also be remembered. In Spanish history the word *moro*, or Moor, is really a blanket term covering not merely the Arabs, who in reality originated from many different regions, but also Berbers and other non-Arabs— all united under the banner of Islam.

Abd al-Rahman III himself reflected the wonderfully mixed identity that was being forged out of the various cultures and peoples of the peninsula. His mother was a Christian concubine, most probably from the Basque region, his grandfather was the son of an Arab emir of Cordoba, and his grandmother was a Christian princess who had been sent by her father, the King of Navarre in the north, as an offering to cement close ties with Al-Andalus. He spoke fluent Arabic as well as the Latin-based language used by the Christians— the precursor of modern Spanish.

Advance of the Christian Kings

The Muslims were destined to fight a long and losing battle to remain in Spain. Throughout the course of the centuries, the northern boundaries with the Christian kingdoms would be wild frontier lands that from the tenth century onwards would move slowly but inexorably down the peninsula, leaving the Muslims with ever-decreasing territory. On the far side of the frontier lay the Christian kingdoms bent on reconquering their old lands, while on the near side were the rebellious Muslim chiefs who were a law unto themselves, lording over the land with their own small armies and demonstrating an alarming tendency to broker private treaties with their Christian neighbors. Order ultimately depended on the large and costly mercenary army maintained by the rulers in Cordoba, the upkeep of which placed extra pressure on the tax-paying population and, on occasion, led to scenes of serious rioting in the capital.

Weakened by continuous warring against the Christians and undermined by power struggles within its own leadership, the Caliphate of Cordoba eventually ground to a halt in the early eleventh century. Al-Andalus disintegrated into a patchwork of small Muslim states known as "taifas," also called "petty kingdoms." There were no less than than twenty-three *taifas* in all—the most powerful of which was Seville, whose rulers were continually at odds with each other.

In such a volatile world, it was up to each *taifa* to decide how best to protect itself and which allies to choose. Often this meant calling on the help of Christians who were only too happy to oblige. This state of virtual anarchy gave the Christian kingdoms, which were already exacting heavy tribute from the bordering northern *taifas* in return for their independence, a perfect opportunity to sack and pillage Muslim towns. Islamic unity was thus dealt a severe blow. From this point forward, the Christians had the upper hand, and the gradual process of the *Reconquista*, or "Reconquest," of the land from the Muslims began in earnest.

The inevitable loss of Toledo in 1085 to the Christians sent shock waves through the Islamic world, an ominous portent of the catastrophe to come. To help launch a counter-offensive, the Muslim emir of Seville appealed for back-up from a fanatical dynasty over the sea in Morocco. These were the Almoravids, a group of warriors who obligingly launched what they saw as a ferocious "jihad" or holy war, and subsequently decided to stay.

The strategy of Seville's emir had fatally backfired. For a while, all of Muslim Spain fell under the sway of these new invaders—a period which saw the persecution of the Jewish and Christian populations. The Almoravids in turn were replaced by another fanatical Moroccan dynasty, the Almohads, who entered Spain in 1146 and established Seville as their capital. The city began to flourish as never before. The Almohads oversaw the construction of palaces, mosques and other buildings as well as renovating the city's river docking facilities, dramatically enhancing its role as a major business center in the Mediterranean world. It was also the Almohads who built the wonderful tower, the Giralda, which still stands today. Such was the splendor of the city that, according to a proverb, even bird's milk could be procured in Seville if so requested.

Muslim Spain Finally Falls

By the thirteenth century, it was clear that the tide had finally turned against the Muslims. In 1236, the once-great city of Cordoba fell to the Kingdom of Castilla-Leon and its Great Mosque was converted into a cathedral, which it remains to this day. It was the bitterest of blows to the Islamic world.

More losses followed rapidly, including Seville in 1248. Prior to its capitulation, the city had languished for two years under siege, until its citizens, starved of food and water, were ordered to leave with only the possessions they could carry, leaving the Christians to an eerie ghost town. For two centuries the last Muslim stronghold was the kingdom of Granada, its capital described by a contemporary Egyptian traveler as one of the "greatest and most beautiful cities." Granada eventually was forced to agree to the terms of peace imposed by the powerful Kingdom of Castilla and to pay tribute.

It was the Nasrids of Granada, the last Muslim dynasty to rule in Spain, who were responsible for the creation of the Alhambra, a complex of palaces that still ranks among the greatest examples of Muslim architecture in Spain, or indeed of any type in the world today.

Statue in Cordoba of Moses ben Maimon ("Maimonides") (1135-1204), the Cordoban-born Jewish scholar, physician, and philosopher. Regarded as the most influential Jewish thinker of the Middle Ages, his works profoundly influenced Christian thought. He was one of many forced to leave Spain to avoid religious persecution at the hands of the fanatical Almohads, eventually reaching Cairo where he served as physician to the sultan of Egypt. He occupies a special place at the crossroad of Greco-Roman, Arab, Jewish, and modern Western thought.

The fifteenth century Catholic super-state, formed by the union of the Kingdoms of Castilla and Aragon through the political marriage of their rulers Queen Isabel and King Fernando, sounded the death knell for Muslim society in Spain. Granada, the final obstacle to long-cherished dreams of a united Catholic Spain, faced an all out attack and inevitably surrendered in 1492, the same year in which Christopher Columbus sailed across the Atlantic on the orders of Queen Isabel and chanced upon the American Continent.

While the church bells rang across Christian Europe, Muslims were left reeling in shock. The unthinkable had happened—eight

JOHN JOYCE

GILLIAN JOYCE

The Architecture of Muslim Spain

Left: The Giralda of Seville. A minaret built by the Almohads in the twelfth century from which to call the faithful to prayer. Inside the tower is a series of gently sloping ramps that permitted two guards to ascend on horseback. Once part of a mosque, after its seizure by Christians in the thirteenth century, it eventually became the tower of the city's cathedral and was modified by successive generations of architects and fitted out with bells.

JOHN JOYCE

GILLIAN JOYCE

Above left and right: Dating mostly from the fourteenth century, the Alhambra takes it name from the Arabic "Al-Qal'a Al-Hamra," meaning "The Red Fortress," after an earlier building that was built on the same site in the ninth century. With the new Alhambra, the Granadan architects created a wonderful interplay between landscape and architecture, setting pavilions and towers against dramatic backdrops of the nearby snow-capped mountain ranges. Other features include stunning interior courtyards, elaborately carved woodwork, and stucco and surfaces adorned with poetic inscriptions.

Right: The interior of the Mosque of Cordoba (now a Catholic cathedral). Begun under Abd al-Rahman I in 785, it features hundreds of pillars supporting red-and-white arches.

Spain—A Catalyst for Western Civilization

During the tenth century, under the patronage of Caliph Abd al-Rahman III—who was determined to show that Cordoba could equal Baghdad in greatness—poets, philosophers, historians, musicians, and scholars were encouraged to settle in Al-Andalus. Islamic Spain now began to develop its own distinct contribution to the world of learning and would play a vital role in the transeference not only only of Islamic scholarship to the West, but also Greek philosophical and scientific works that had long been lost to Christendom. These were works that would stimulate the European Renaissance and directly influence the scientific revolution that would lead to the ascendancy of Europe throughout the world.

The fall of Toledo to the Christians in 1085, while a major blow for the Islamic world, proved to be a priceless jewel for the West. It was here that Western scholars were at last fully able to immerse themelves the world of Muslim learning. Where the Greek Classics had previously been translated into Arabic and preserved by Muslim scholars, now in Toledo the very same works as well as Arabic texts on mathematics, astronomy, philosophy, and other subjects began to be translated into Latin for Western consumption. Jewish scholars, with their knowledge of both Arabic and Latin, played a vital role in the process. A key figure in the translation movement in Toledo was Gerard of Cremona (*c.* 1114-87) who, dissatisfied with the meager offerings of European learning, went to Toledo in order to learn Arabic so that he might be able to access the wealth of the great Islamic libraries. Under the tutorship of a native Christian writer, Ibn Ghalib, Gerard managed to master the language and translated into Latin more than seventy works that included works by Hippocrates, Aristotle and Ptolemy as well as the Medical Canon of Ibn Sina (Avicenna) and the surgical works of Al-Zahrawi (Albucasis), both of them Muslim scholars without rival.

Cordoba was the birthplace of the great Islamic philosopher Ibn Rushd (1126-1198), also known by his Latin name Averroes. His commentaries on Aristotle profoundly influenced both Muslim and Christian thinkers in Medieval times, including St. Thomas Aquinas. Many of his books were translated into Latin, Hebrew, German, and English. Christopher Columbus credited him as one of the thinkers who helped him to predict the existence of the New World.

Spain also appears to have been one of the earliest routes for introduction into Europe of the concept of zero, decimalization, and Arabic numerical figures (replacing the cumbersome Roman numerals). The person popularly credited for successfully introducing this was Gerbert (*c.* 945-1003), who later became Pope Sylvester II. He was a classic example of this cross-fertilization of ideas. Born in France, Gerbert entered the service of the Roman Catholic Church and subsequently spent time studying in Spain under Muslim teachers in Cordoba and Seville, where he excelled in mathematics and the natural sciences.

centuries of unparalleled Islamic civilization in Spain had been brought to an end. It would leave a permanent sense of loss among the Muslims, one that is still keenly felt today.

While a period of cooling off followed the fall of Granada, Muslims, who had initially been guaranteed certain rights, including freedom of worship and the right to trade under the peace treaty, were now becoming the focus of persecution. Under the new order in Spain it soon became clear that there would be no room for religious non-conformity. In an act that has been likened by some to ethnic cleansing, both Muslims—now known as *mudéjares*, meaning "those who stayed"—and Jews remaining in Spain were given the stark choice of conversion or expulsion. Many chose to leave.

Mosque entrance in Cordoba.

As it turned out, large numbers of Jews found safety in the Muslim Ottoman Empire. Others even went north to less hostile centers in Europe such as Amsterdam. Their culture and Ladino language also went with them. What Yiddish was to the European Ashkenazi Jews, Ladino was to the Jews of medieval Spain and their descendants, known as the Sephardim (from *Sefarad* the Hebrew word meaning Spain.) Also known as Judesco or Judaeo-Spanish, Ladino began as a variant of old Spanish, but soon developed a life of its own. In Istanbul, once the capital of the Ottoman Empire and now the modern state of Turkey, there still exists a sizable community of Jews of Spanish origin who speak this language.

Many Jews of this diaspora moved closer to home, sailing for the shores of North Africa with the few possessions they were allowed to take with them. Even today, it is possible to find houses in Morocco owned by Jewish families who proudly show, hanging on their wall, the door-key to the home in Spain from which their ancestors fled.

For those who remained, conversion to Christianity by no means guaranteed safety. Deeply distrusted, converts from Islam and Judaism were to face one of the most notorious institutions ever established in the name of religion, a name that has become synonymous with torture, intolerance, and injustice—the Spanish Inquisition.

Where once Muslims, Jews and Christians had flourished under the laws of Islam and had made Al-Andalus synonymous with tolerance and learning, now academic books, once so highly prized, were heaped into piles on the streets and burned by fanatical Christian clergymen. By the beginning of the seventeenth century, it was clear that there was no longer a place for those of Muslim descent in Spain. The country's remaining Moorish population, numbering as many as 300,000, many of them skilled farmers who played an important part in the country's economy, were unceremoniously thrown out of Spain. Neither Muslims, nor indeed Jews, would officially be allowed back into Spain until the nineteenth century.

This hostility was taken up in much of the rest of Europe. In 1530, for example, when the Arabic text of the Qur'an was published by Christians in Venice in the name of enlightenment and scholarship, Pope Paul III gave orders that all copies were to be burned. An era of mutual understanding had ended.

A fourteenth-century Nasrid
woven silk fabric from
Southern Spain or North Africa.

The Mysticism
of the Sufis

"On the day that you were born,
A ladder was placed
To help you leave this world."
—Rumi, Sufi mystic

Throughout its history, Islam, like Christianity and other mainstream religions, has enjoyed a rich and profoundly influential tradition of mysticism. Mystics of Islam came to be known as Sufis, a name traditionally believed to have derived from the Arabic word for wool, *suf*, from the fact that some of their number dressed in simple white, woolen garments.

Parting with mainstream Islam, Sufis were little concerned with religious dogma. Their view held that individuals did not have to put their lives on hold and wait for the death of the body to experience direct communion with God. Such a state could be attained, at least partially, in the here and now. Achievement of this state required of the seeker a sustained and skillful effort to transcend the self's fixations with the details, impulses, and dramas of everyday life, and to allow it to become absorbed into a greater unified reality—a state that was no less than a realization of the oneness of God. A central practice in Sufi orders was the "recollection" or *dhikr* of God, which could take a variety of meditation forms such as movement or chanting.

The way of the Sufi was not an intellectual undertaking but one that came from the heart, the love of God being the potent force that could enable the soul to rediscover its divine source and be reunited with the truth.

The following verses by the great Sufi poet, Jalal al-Din Rumi (1207-1273) capture the intensity of the mystic's need to surrender the false self in order to to attain spiritual fulfillment:

For a while, as was my habit
I looked for my self;
Though I did not see my true self
I heard its name.

Being a prisoner of myself,
I did not deserve my true self
Until I abandoned my self
And so found my true self.

Sufi practices, rituals, and teachings were as numerous as the Sufi schools and traditions that came and went. In the early years Islamic mysticism was pioneered by highly charismatic individuals, whose lives were characterized by austerity and rigorous discipline. Among these were Hasan al-Basri, Al-Muhasib and Al-Junayd—the latter an especially important figure in the formative period of Islamic mystical thought.

Rabia—A Life of Devotion

Women also played an important role in the tradition; among them was Rabia al-Adawiyya, regarded as a saint and considered to rank amongst the greatest teachers in Sufi history. The details of Rabia's life are extremely hazy. An inhabitant of Basra (today in Iraq), she is believed to have been born in 717 and died in 801. According to tradition she came from a poor family and was enslaved after the death of her parents. Later freed under miraculous circumstances, she lived her days in poverty and self-denial—it is said that her only possessions were a broken jug to drink from, an old reed mat to sit on, and a brick for a pillow.

Her life encapsulated the Sufi theme of love and was entirely devoted to God. Not surprisingly therefore, she never married and after being asked if she would ever do so is said to have replied: "The marriage knot can only tie one who exists. Where is existence here? I am not my own. I am His and at His command. You should seek permission from Him."

Whereas other mystics had dedicated their lives to God out of fear, Rabia brought to the Sufi tradition the potent idea that God should be loved for God's sake alone:

If I adore You out of fear of Hell, burn me in Hell!
If I adore You out of desire for Paradise,
Lock me out of Paradise.
But if I adore You for Yourself alone,
Do not deny to me Your eternal beauty!

When asked why she had walked through the streets of Basra with a torch in one hand and a bucket of water in the other, she is reported to have replied:

I carry a torch in one hand
And a bucket of water in the other.
With these things I am going to set fire to Heaven
And put out the flames of Hell
So that voyagers to God can rip the veils
And see the real goal.

Growth of Sufism

Individuals like Rabia exerted an enormous influence on the formation of the Islamic mystical tradition. In time, Sufis would organize themselves into distinctive schools and orders, based on the teachings of highly respected spiritual teachers, many of whom became regarded as saints and whose writings would come to gain respect across the Muslim world. Once accepted into one of these orders, the disciple or *murid* would follow the teachings and example of the master closely for the rest of his or her life.

Among the earliest of these movements was Jalal al-Din Rumi's Mawlawiyya order, founded in the fourteenth century and based in Konya, Turkey. Using dance and singing in their

Whirling dervishes, or sufis.

85

rituals their members became known as "whirling dervishes" in the West. As Rumi said:

> The music inside we do not often hear,
> But still we all dance to it!

Sufi orders usually encouraged their members to participate in worldly activities—in taking jobs, for example—rather than withdrawing into monastic seclusion. Additionally, there was no culture of chastity found in the monastic orders of Christianity— a concept generally frowned upon in Islam. While there were many examples of Sufis taking the vow of poverty, Sufi movements could be quite wealthy, taking on forms of organization not unlike the freemasonry that was developing in Europe.

Ultimately, following the Sufi way was a personal quest, an undertaking to understand, experience, and integrate one's being into the divine reality of existence. Such an inward search necessarily entailed non-conformity to orthodox interpretations of Islam, putting it at odds with the religious establishment, which was of the view that those sincerely wishing to seek spiritual fulfillment should dedicate their lives only to the study of the Qur'an, Hadiths, and Sharia law.

Disapproval sometimes turned to persecution and the Sufi community produced its fair share of martyrs. A famous example was Al-Hallaj, a Sufi who traveled extensively throughout Central Asia and India and had become a popular teacher. Born in Iran in 858, Al-Hallaj was considered an "intoxicated Sufi," who became so enraptured in ecstasy by the presence of the Divine that he was prone to a loss of personal identity, which blurs the lines between the Divine and Man. His profound mystical experiences led him to declare: "I have seen my Lord with the eye of my heart, and I said: 'Who are You?' He said: 'You.' "

These spells of ecstasy led him to make the fateful utterance: "*Ana al-haqq!*" or "I am the Truth!"—words that could also be interpreted in Islam as very clearly meaning "I am God!" He was thrown into prison for eleven years in Baghdad. His views were condemned by jurists as heretical, and he was finally brutally tortured and crucified. Witnesses state that the mystic was strangely serene throughout his ordeal, and forgave his persecutors before he expired.

Despite the controversy that surrounds the Sufi tradition, it is nevertheless an integral part of Islam and emphasizes the centrality of the Muslim belief in One God, the Qur'an, and the legitimacy of the Prophet Muhammad, whom they consider their model teacher. The very elusiveness of their mysticism, combined with their unquestionable belief in the Qur'an and Muhammad's mission, always made it hard to take seriously charges made against them of heresy. Such charges were more likely to stem from political factors rather than religious. In fact, the Sufis' spiritual commitment and example, accompanied by a rich body of literature, has earned them a great deal of respect across the Muslim world, albeit often grudgingly.

One individual who did much to boost the reputation of the Sufis was Al-Ghazali (*d.* 1111), one of the most influential figures in Islam. Al-Ghazali turned to the mystic path after realizing that his spiritual yearnings could not be satisfied exclusively by the kind of rational inquiry undertaken by the orthodox scholars. He declared:

> I knew that the complete mystic "way" includes both intellectual belief and practical activity. The latter consists of getting rid of the obstacles in the self and of stripping its base characteristics and vicious mores, so that the heart may attain to freedom from what is not God and to constant recollection of Him.

In his works he was able to reconcile some of the differences between mystical and scholastic aspects of Islam in a way that was acceptable to many. After his death, Sufism began to gain ground, spreading rapidly throughout the Islamic world, and throughout the centuries it remained a spiritual resource that Muslims everywhere have tapped to some degree.

The Sufis were the indefatigable yet often overlooked force behind the spread and maintenance of Islam in many parts of the world. From West Africa to Central Asia or India to Indonesia, the presence of Sufi teachers was never far. By appealing to the spiritual side of human nature and dispensing with dogma, they were able to bridge the gap between Islam and local religious customs and beliefs. Converts were won over not by force, but by the example they set. Even in cases where Islam failed to dislodge local religious customs and beliefs, Sufis were often revered as holy men, their message recognized as transcending religious divisions.

The Legacy of the Sufis

Sufis are very much alive and active in the modern world, presenting their most visible side with their music and dances, and in some cases attracting a huge following that is normally reserved for pop stars. An example is Pakistan-born Nusrat Fateh Ali Khan (1948-1997) whose haunting and improvised devotional music, rooted firmly in the tradition of Qawwali, achieved such popularity, leading to international record sales and highly successful concerts around the world, including Europe and the United States. The roots of Qawwali can be traced back many centuries to Persian spiritual songs, and its devotional themes of love and peace are held to derive from God.

The whirling dervishes have also attracted a great deal of attention in the West, and dances such as the those performed for visitors at the Mausoleum of Al-Ghouri in Cairo continue to fascinate audiences. The dancers, accompanied by musicians, rotate in a trancelike way; their ultimate aim is to enter into an ecstatic state. As their speed increases, the folds of their skirt-like garments rise outwards, creating a swirl of colors to mesmerizing effect.

> The hidden revolution inside us
> Causes the whole universe revolve.
> Our heads not heeding our feet, nor our feet our heads.
> Neither knows the other
> But still they keep revolving.

Modern Sufi thinkers, such as the great Idries Shah (1924-1996), have enriched the libraries of the world with their writings that present the tradition to a fresh audience, highlighting often surprising similarities between Sufism and other non-Muslim forms of mysticism and spiritual thought. Meanwhile, the old Sufi masters continue to be revered as great saints and their tombs are major places of pilgrimage.

The Crusades

"The sultan sat with his face gleaming with happiness. His seat looked as if it were surrounded by the halo of the moon and around him were readers of the Qur'an and poets reciting and seeking favors. Flags were unfurled and pens sharpened to convey the good tidings. Eyes were filled with tears of joy while hearts were humbled in devotion to God and in joy for the victory."
—Imad al-Din, Muslim chronicler, witnessing Saladin's recapture of Jerusalem

Shortly after the loss of Toledo in 1085 to the Spanish Christians the Islamic world was confronted with another devastating blow—this time at the other end of the Mediterranean. Within a matter of years, the third most holy city in Islam, Jerusalem, along with a significant part of Syria and Palestine, had been seized by a huge allied army of Christian Crusaders from Europe. It would take nearly two centuries for the Muslims to complete their own reconquest and bring the region squarely back under the banner of Islam.

Between the eleventh and fourteenth centuries, the Europeans launched nine Crusades against the Muslims in the Holy Land. These campaigns were in fact part of a broader and protracted struggle between Christians and Muslims. Within Europe itself, the Western Christians were seeking to consolidate their power by engaging in a myriad of other "holy" wars aimed at the enemies of the Church, including the Muslims in Spain and, later, the Ottomans in the Balkans.

The First Crusade in the Middle East was the one that successfully launched the Christians into the Holy Land. Taking advantage of Muslim disunity, the Christians were able to establish four Crusader states in Syria and Palestine—the Kingdom of Jerusalem, the County of Tripoli, the Principality of Antioch, and the County of Edessa.

The Crusade originally began as a response to an appeal for help by the Byzantine Emperor Alexius I in Constantinople in driving out the Seljuk Turks who had overrun his eastern territories. In Rome, Pope Urban II, anxious to display the power of the papacy, heeded this call to save Eastern Christendom from the Muslims.

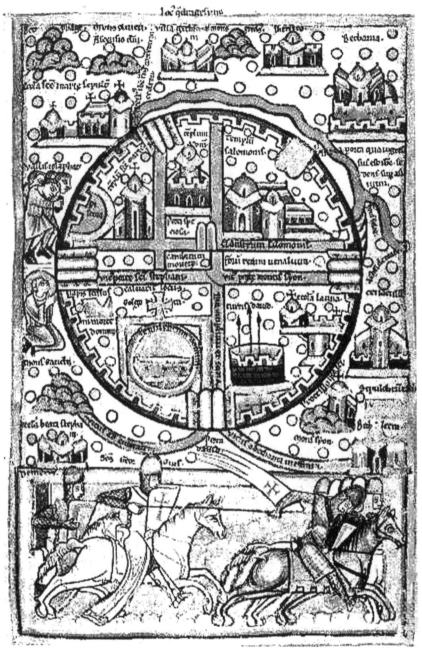

Early Crusader map of Jerusalem.

On November 26, 1095, in a speech made in southern France, Urban urged all Western Christians to defend the Eastern Church and "enter upon the road to the Holy Sepulcher and wrest it from the wicked race and subject it." The Holy Sepulcher was a cave in Jerusalem where the body of Christ was believed to have lain before his Resurrection and was marked by a church. The Christian world had earlier been outraged at the church's destruction by the Fatimid Caliph Al-Hakim in 1010.

Emperor Alexius got far more than he bargained for. Within a year, an army of 150,000 had gathered in Constantinople, ready to march against the Muslims. Yet the Orthodox Christians of the East were far from happy with the idea of a Crusade organized by the Catholic Papacy. From the outset the Easterners would view the Western Crusaders with deep suspicion, fearing they cared little about helping ward off the Turks, but instead harbored ambitions to seize the wealth of Constantinople, famed as "the richest city in the world."

In fact, the Byzantines, with their own distinct Eastern Orthodox interpretation of Christianity, were at odds with Western Europe over important issues relating to faith. Futhermore, considering themselves to be the true heirs of the Roman Empire, they had a distinctly unflattering view of the Franks (the blanket term used for all Christians of Western Europe), whom they considered little more than uncivilized brutes. Capturing the feeling of the time, Princess Anna Comnena (1083-d. after 1148), an outstanding historian who was also the daughter of Emperor Alexius, disparagingly dismissed the visitors as uncultured barbarians who were beneath both the Byzantines and Muslims in terms of intelligence and refinement.

Anna Comnena summed up her father's concerns:

> The rumor that innumerable Frankish armies were approaching came to the Emperor's ears. He dreaded their arrival, for he knew their impetuosity, their unstable and fickle character, and indeed everything about the Celtic temperament and its inevitable consequences. He knew how grasping the sight of riches made them and that at the first opportunity they would violate their treaties without scruple.

The Byzantines certainly had good cause for concern. The Papacy saw in the conquest of the Holy Land an opportunity to unite

Western Europe under its own rule by giving the feuding and fractious nobility of kings, princes, and robber barons the excuse to join forces in a common goal.

The army of Crusaders turned out to be a rather worrisome hodgepodge of Europeans from all walks of life, from the lowliest peasants to members of the nobility. Among their ranks were romantics, adventurers, and criminals, lured by dreams of making their fortunes overseas, or, for some, of dying a martyr's death. Furthermore, before their arrival in Constantinople, Crusader forces had already gained some notoriety from incidents where Jews in Germany and France were robbed and assaulted, and a general pillaging spree across the Balkans. Emperor Alexius was forced to acknowledge the fact that he was ultimately powerless to control the Crusades, and instead focused his energies on limiting the damage and maximizing any gains to be had—contenting himself with regaining Byzantine control over the western coast of Anatolia.

Once the Crusaders were unleashed in the Middle East, they found no united Muslim front to impede their advance. By now, having reached the limits of its expansion, the Islamic world was in disarray and the Middle East lay divided. In control of Palestine were the Shi'i Fatimids, major rivals of the Abbasid Caliphs of Baghdad who themselves had surrendered their once great political powers to the Turkish Seljuk sultans. Meanwhile, Syria had been parceled out between rival Seljuk Atabegs and Turkish Emirs.

The Crusaders had few problems in reaching their goal, the Holy City of Jerusalem. Having gained extensive territories along the Eastern Mediterranean, in the summer of 1099 they amassed a force of some 20,000 men outside the gates of the prized city. The Egyptian Fatimid force entrusted with protecting Jerusalem numbered no more than a thousand, and so they stood little chance. After a month's siege, the Crusaders came storming through the city walls and embarked on an orgy of violence. They butchered thousands of people, Muslims, Jews, and native Christians alike. The defeat, and the dreadful manner in which it was carried out, would leave a long-lasting feeling of bitterness among Muslims.

Having seized the prize of Jerusalem, the Crusaders set about strengthening their position in the Middle East, carving their new territories into four separate states, including the Kingdom of Jerusalem, which stretched all the way south to the Red Sea.

Saladin and the Recapture of Jerusalem

One of the greatest Muslim heroes of all time, Salah al-Din, earned his reputation fighting the Crusaders. Better known to the Western world as Saladin, he was a brilliant military commander who possessed a deep sense of honor that impressed even his greatest enemies. His firm yet just leadership helped unite the Muslims against Christian Europe, winning back for them the Holy City of Jerusalem after nearly ninety years of occupation under the Crusaders.

Saladin was born to a Kurdish family in 1138, in Tikrit, which lies on the Tigris River in northern present-day Iraq. Though little is known of Saladin's early life, he was quite familiar with both the Turkic and Arabic cultures that were dominant in his day. As a youth he appears to have been taken by the study of the Qur'an and poetry, and throughout his life he remained rigorously orthodox in his religious convictions.

At the age of eighteen, Saladin was made deputy military governor of Damascus, a job that involved maintaining law and order. Subsequently, he participated in successful campaigns against the Crusaders in Egypt, alongside his uncle, Shirkuh, in 1169, and, at the age of thirty-one, rose to become vizier of Egypt, assuming greater military powers in the process. He was now in a position to achieve two highly significant acts in Islamic history. The first was to restore Sunnism to Egypt after two centuries of Shi'i rule under the Fatimids, and the second was to reclaim Jerusalem for Islam.

The Fatimid Caliph's death in 1171 gave Saladin the chance to stage a quiet religious coup, spelling the beginning of the end for Shi'ism in Egypt. He had the traditional mention of the Caliph's name dropped from prayers in the mosques on Friday, the Muslim holy day of the week, and replaced by that of the Abbasid Caliph. With this simple act, he had begun the process of bringing the country back to the path of Sunni orthodoxy.

In 1174, Saladin gained control over Syria, and turned his attention to the question of the Christian Crusaders. After a series of successful campaigns, in July 1187 he launched his most ambitious offensive against the European invaders and crushed a huge Crusader army at the Battle of Hattin in northern Palestine. Having inflicted a massive physical and psychological blow on his enemy, the prize was now ready for the taking. On October 2, after a siege of only one week, the city of Jerusalem surrendered. Fortunately for its inhabitants, Saladin chose not to repeat the violent abuses carried out by the Crusaders years earlier, and Christians were allowed to leave peacefully. Further victories followed in the wake of this devastating blow, and the Crusader towns fell, one by one, until only a handful remained.

Saladin— One of history's greatest military leaders.

The loss of Jerusalem predictably sent shockwaves throughout Europe, and there was no shortage of men to willing to join the third and largest of the Crusades. It was here that Saladin was to pit his wits against another legendary warrior of the time, Richard I ("Lionheart") of England. The latest Crusaders concentrated their efforts on the coastal city of Acre (today in Israel), laying siege to it by land and sea. In July 1191, after two long years, Saladin's forces finally surrendered the city to the Crusaders. Yet, not for the want of trying, the English king never succeeded in capturing Jerusalem. Instead Richard the Lionheart was forced to make a truce with Saladin. In the resulting peace talks, it was agreed that the Crusaders would keep control of some of the coastal territories, while the Muslims would retain the interior lands and their cities, and permit Christians safe access to the holy pilgrim sites.

Months after peace was restored in the Middle East, Saladin was struck down by fever. He died on March 4, 1193, at the age of 55. It was said that in his final moments he had a smile on his face that anticipated paradise. He was buried in Damascus.

Saladin's successors, the Ayyubids, continued to maintain Egypt's importance in the Muslim world, at least for a while. Despite periods of political turmoil, the dynasty went on to achieve a series of successes against the Crusaders. This was especially so in the case of the Sixth Crusade, which suffered a crushing defeat at the hands of the Egyptians.

This ill-fated Crusader army optimistically had marched into Egypt only to be defeated at Cairo in April 1250. They suffered the further humiliation of seeing their leader, King Louis IX of France, taken hostage along with many of his nobles, and held for ransom for a million gold dinars. Only after the enormous sum was paid was the unfortunate king released.

The Ayyubids also oversaw a period of economic and cultural revival in Egypt. Furthermore, as Shi'i institutions were systematically replaced with those of the Sunni rite, thus eradicating Fatimid influence, orthodox Sunnism took firm root, and it remains the dominant form of Islam in Egypt to this day. To this end, the Ayyubids founded numerous *madrasas*—the religious schools that became the cornerstone of spiritual life in Egypt. The Ayubbids themselves were destined to come to an ignominious end at the hands of the sultan's own personal elite corps, the ranks of which were made up of specially imported slaves known as Mamluks.

Muslim-Christian Relations

Despite the generally hostile climate between Muslims and Crusaders, at a more local level both sides often took a highly pragmatic approach with regard to their dealings with one another. Diplomatic relations were maintained and treaties regularly made between the two sides in the Middle East, as indeed had been happening for many years at the other end of the Mediterranean in Spain. In fact, those Christians who had settled in the land and had adapted to their new way of life were far from happy about newcomers coming in and stirring up trouble. Trade remained an important priority and both sides invested a good amount of effort to secure stable enough conditions for it to prosper, and prosper it did.

In his memoirs, the Syrian Arab, Osama, noted how some Westerners had even begun to adopt Middle Eastern customs:

> There are some Franks who have settled in our land and taken to living like Muslims. These are better than those who have just arrived from their homelands, but they are the exception and cannot be take as typical.

Osama further recounted how a friend of his was invited to dine at the house of a retired Crusader knight in Antioch who employed Egyptian cooks and, eschewing Frankish food, ate only what they ate—"No pig's flesh ever comes into my house!" he exclaimed.

In the late twelfth century, the traveler Ibn Jubayr vividly described the bustling trade he saw in one part of the region:

> Acre is the capital of the Frankish cities in Syria, the unloading place of ships, reared aloft in the seas like mountains and a port of call for all ships. In its greatness it resembles Constantinople. It is the focus of ships and caravans and the meeting place of Muslim and Christian merchants from all regions.

Witnessing the caravans of the spice trade making their way from India via the ports of Yemen and Aydhab on the Red Sea coast, Ibn Jubayr marveled that "the greater part of this was the loads of pepper, so numerous as to seem to our fancy to equal in quantity only dust!"

Chroniclers on both sides enjoyed using pejorative terms when referring to each other—Christian writers referred to the Muslims as "Saracen dogs," the Muslims in turn branded them "Christian swine." Nevertheless, there were numerous instances of mutual admiration. Saladin for one was admired by the Franks, and several of his counterparts in turn earned the respect of the Muslims. Richard the Lionheart, for example, was described by the Muslim chronicler Ibn al-Athir as:

> . . . the Man of his Age as regards courage, shrewdness, endurance and forbearance . . . because of him the Muslims were sorely tested by unprecedented disaster.

Another leader held in high esteem by Muslim chroniclers was the colorful and controversial Frederick II of Hohenstaufen (1194-1250), King of Sicily, Jerusalem, and the Holy Roman Emperor. Brought up in Sicily, which between the ninth and eleventh centuries had been under Muslim rule, Frederick II was exposed at an early age to the strong Islamic culture that persisted on the island, and retained a interest in Islam and Arabic into his adult life. He welcomed Muslims as much as Christians and Jews at his court and kept a personal bodyguard of Muslim soldiers.

Suspecting his true loyalties, a succession of Catholic Popes even referred to him as a "baptized sultan," and excommunicated him. Writing of Frederick in 1228, Ibn Wasil, a Mamluk envoy from Egypt, said:

> Amongst the kings of the Franks, the Emperor was outstanding, a lover of wisdom, logic, and medicine, inclining towards the Muslims because his place of origin and upbringing was Sicily and he and his father and his grandfather were its kings and the majority of the island are Muslims.

Frederick established a particularly close rapport with the Ayyubid sultan, Al-Malik al-Kamil, who had signed a peace treaty surrendering Jerusalem to him in 1229. He sent the Sultan complex mathematical and philosophical problems that the latter eagerly set about trying to solve with the help of whole teams of Muslim scholars.

A Christian and a Muslim playing chess
in the thirteenth century.

From Mongols
to Mamluks

"Stories have been related to me, which the hearer can scarcely credit, as to the terror of the Tatars, which God Almighty cast into men's hearts, so that it is said that a single one of them would enter a village or quarter wherein were many people, and would continue to slay them one after another, none daring to stretch forth his hand against this horseman."
—*Ibn al-Athir, Arab Historian (1160-1233)*

While the invasion of the Middle East by the Crusaders was a major blow to the Muslim world, it nevertheless served to galvanize Muslims into action, giving them a cause in which they could unite. It produced heroes and yielded great victories, yet in the eyes of Muslim chroniclers it was never considered as important as the events that were to unfold during the first quarter of the thirteenth century with the arrival of an utterly different kind of foe—the Mongols.

Unlike the Christians, the pagan Mongols appeared utterly alien, brutal, and terrifying. Seemingly from nowhere, these nomads appeared like wildfire, mercilessly destroying whole villages, towns, and cities that showed the least sign of resistance.

The Mongol onslaught was fully unleashed in 1219, when the great leader Genghis Khan, having united the Mongol tribes of the east, invaded Central Asia. Bukhara, one of the principal centers of theological study in the Islamic world, was devastated with most of its mosques, academies, and bazaars left in ruins. So too was the other great central Asian city of Samarkand. The damage was such that when the Tunisian traveler Ibn Battuta visited Bukhara in the mid-fourteenth century he felt compelled to lament that "there is not one of its inhabitants today who possesses any theological learning or makes any attempt to learn it."

The Mongol invasion so profoundly affected the Arab historian Ibn al-Athir (1160-1233), who had described the invasions to date as "the greatest calamity that had befallen mankind," that he was scarcely able to put pen to paper:

> For some years I continued averse from mentioning this event, deeming it so horrible that I shrank from recording it and ever withdrawing one foot as I advanced the other. To whom, indeed, can it be easy to write the announcement of the death-blow of Islam and the Muslims, or who is he on whom the remembrance thereof can weigh lightly? O would that my mother had not borne me or that I had died and become a forgotten thing ere this befell! Yet, withal a number of my friends urged me to set it down in writing, and I hesitated long, but at last came to the conclusion that to omit this matter could serve no useful purpose.

The Fall of Baghdad

Genghis Khan's empire soon broke up into a number of states ruled by dynasties established by his many descendants. One of these was a grandson, Hulegu, who struck Islamic civilization one of its greatest blows, with the capture of Baghdad itself, popularly believed to be impregnable.

Hulegu's assault on Baghdad came in 1258, after the city proudly refused to surrender. What followed was an orgy of gratuitous brutality and destruction that left the Muslim world profoundly traumatized. Hulegu, whose mother and wife were both Nestorian Christians, was a shamanist with Buddhist sympathies. He showed little mercy to Muslims. On capturing the city, he let his men butcher thousands upon thousands of the city's Muslim inhabitants—the Jews and Christians were fortunate to be spared the same fate.

The Mongols left the bloodstained capital in ruins—its palaces, mosques and other institutions utterly destroyed. After forcing the reigning Caliph, Musta'sim, to reveal where he had hidden his royal treasure, the Mongols had him stitched into a carpet and trampled to death under the hooves of their horses. It was a carefully chosen method of death. As the historian Sir Thomas W. Arnold noted:

> The awe with which the institution of the Caliphate was regarded, even in these days of its weakness, may be realized

by the fact that cruel and bloodthirsty savage though Hulegu was, even he hesitated to put to death the successor of the Prophet, for the Muhammadans who accompanied him in his army in the expedition against Baghdad had warned him that if the blood of the Caliph was shed upon the ground the world would be overspread with darkness and the army of the Mongols be swallowed up by an earthquake.

At prayers offered in the great mosque of Baghdad on the Friday following the death of the Caliph, the mood was summed up by the following lament:

Praise be to God who has caused exalted personages to perish and has given over to destruction the inhabitants of this city! O God, help us in our misery, the like of which Islam and its children have never witnessed; we are God's and unto God we do return!

After the carnage in Baghdad, the Mongols rode on to Damascus, with their sights on Egypt. When it seemed that they were about to overrun the Middle East, it fell to a group of Muslim warriors based in Egypt, whose ferocity was matched by formidable military skills and an unshakable camaraderie, to launch a counterattack.

These were the Mamluks (from the Arabic *mamluk* meaning "owned" or "possessed"), slaves of foreign birth who had traditionally been used by the Ayyubids as an elite military force. They were highly trained cavalrymen, whose skills in archery made them a formidable opponent in the battlefield.

Ascendancy of the Mamluks

The novice Mamluks were converted to Islam and put through a grueling and often dangerous training regime that lasted up to ten years. They learned the art of controlling a horse using their knees, thus leaving their hands free to fire arrows at targets, which they could do seated, and facing the front or the back. In order to build up their arm muscles they would be required to slice lumps of clay up to a thousand times a day with their swords. Polo was also an activity employed to develop their considerable riding skills. Once they had successfully completed their training, the young slaves were given their freedom and could look forward to a comfortable future in the ranks of the ruling elite, some becoming extremely wealthy in the process.

The Mongols had to contend with the ruthless Mamluk leader Baybars, a giant who sported a cataract in one of his blue eyes. It was Baybars, destined to become the first great Mamluk Sultan, who would be remembered in history as the man who put an end to Mongol expansion in the Middle East. In 1260, while Hulegu was distracted elsewhere by a succession struggle between his brothers, Baybars led an army into Syria and defeated the Mongol army there at the Battle of Ayn Jalut. For centuries after his death, the Mamluk warlord remained a popular folk hero whose exploits were mythologized in colorfully exaggerated tales of bravery.

Nevertheless, the damage to the Muslim world had been done. The Mongols had wrought enough havoc on medieval Islamic culture to ensure it would never recover. After five hundred years as the seat of the Abbasid Caliphate, Baghdad's history as a great political and cultural center was over.

Hulegu himself succeeded in building another empire, centered on his capital Tabriz (today in northwestern Iran). Known as the Il-Khanate, it incorporated Persia, Iraq, Anatolia, and the lands reaching north to the Caucasus. Elsewhere across Central Asia new Mongol dynasties created by his cousins emerged.

For all the destruction they caused, the Mongols did eventually go some way in making amends. While the immediate descendants of Hulegu were mostly Buddhists, by the end of the thirteenth century the Il-Khanid ruler Ghazan Khan (r: 1295-1304) officially adopted Islam.

Additionally, the Il-Khanids proved themselves to be great patrons of the arts. Ghazan Khan and his successors actively set about constructing and repairing mosques their predecessors had destroyed. The economy of the region also rallied and Tabriz, now the capital of Iran, became a flourishing trade center that linked Europe and Baghdad, the Persian Gulf and India. Elsewhere other Mongol khans converted to Islam, making their own unique contributions to Islamic culture.

New Defenders of the Sunni World

Meanwhile, after murdering the Sultan, Baybars took the title for himself, and set about strengthening his power. Quick to seize the opportunity, the Mamluk commander legitimized his rule by rescuing the uncle of the murdered Abbasid Caliph and declaring him Caliph in Cairo. But from this point forward, the Caliphs would be mere figureheads, answerable to the Mamluks alone.

Mamluk Egypt now became the major power that linked the East with the West. By defeating the Mongols, assuming the role of Protectors of the Holy Cities of Mecca and Medina, and maintaining the descendants of the Abbasid Caliphate as religious figureheads in Cairo, the canny Mamluks came to be seen as the leading power in the Sunni world. Not only did the Mamluks continue to keep the Mongols at bay, they also took it on themselves to put an end to the Crusader states, which by the end of the thirteenth century had crumbled.

For 250 years the Mamluks were the indisputable masters of Egypt, ruling over one of the most war-torn and troubled regions of those times. Never very many in number, they relied upon their formidable military skills to maintain their success. The Mamluks themselves continued to import slaves, replenishing their ranks with raw recruits. Such an unusual practice worked in the Mamluks' favor. Uprooted from their homes at a young age and with no attachment to the unfamiliar land, the recruits soon developed a fierce loyalty to their masters and comrades in arms.

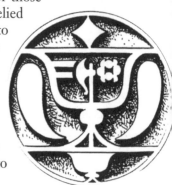

Mamluk heraldic devices.

During the early part of their rule at least,

under the stronger government of the earlier Sultans, Egypt enjoyed periods of prosperity. Soon after Baybars' death in 1277, another Mamluk leader by the name of Qalawun established a new dynasty that was to last for a century. Like Baybars, Qalawun earned a reputation for his military successes against the Mongols and the Christian Crusader states, the latter of which he reduced to a small territory surrounding Acre. The job was finished by his son and successor Khalil, who in 1293 had the last of the beleaguered Crusaders scurrying off in full retreat to the island Kingdom of Cyprus.

Although another of Qalawun's sons, Al-Nasir Muhammad, managed a fairly lengthy, if not continuous, reign between 1294 and 1340, from this time on the ruling elite became decidedly unruly. The following series of Sultans were unable to disentangle themselves from the extremely fractious politics of the time, which was characterized by intense rivalry that often led to bitter and murderous feuds. Indeed, during two-and-a-half centuries of their rule, twenty out of a total of fifty-four Mamluk Sultans came to a violent end, either murdered or executed. Of the rest only ten saw through their natural days in office; the remainder were deposed. Around them powerful and murderous Emirs or Princes fought each other for power, turning the Sultans themselves into little more than puppets.

Cairo Becomes the Center of a Cultural Revival

The Mamluks injected a vigor of their own into the cultural life of Egypt, founding a wonderful legacy of architecture in Cairo that included mosques, mausoleums, forts, and "caravanserais"—the name given to an inn built around a large court that accommodated caravans in the Middle and Far East.

Both Qalawun and his successor Muhammad al-Nasir proved to be important patrons of architecture. So too did Sultan Hassan, who reigned between 1347 and 1361, and whose mosque is considered to among the finest built by the Mamluks and one of Cairo's greatest monuments.

Ultimately, the Mamluks' undoing came from their stubborn refusal to keep up with the times. For more than 250 years, they had successfully managed to use their military skills to keep themselves in power. First and foremost cavalrymen, they had certainly proved themselves to be amongst the finest of their age, but they had only a limited knowledge of the most modern weapons of war—firearms and artillery. Furthermore, they were loath to use them and even went so far as to dismiss guns as a cowardly choice of weapon. When they finally found themselves confronted by the might of the expanding Ottoman Empire, a Muslim state built by Turks on the ashes of Byzantium, they proved to be no match for its well-equipped and well-trained army.

Their death blow finally came in 1516, after the Ottomans defeated the Mamluks at the Battle of Marj Dabiq in Syria. The Mamluks were slaughtered by the Ottoman guns before they could even engage the enemy. The following year, in January 1517, the Ottomans entered Cairo and executed the Sultan. The Mamluks could do little but accept the authority of the new invaders, yet they were by no means finished, and would continue to play a key role in governing the country on behalf of the Ottoman sultans.

Timur—A Resurgence of Mongol and Turkic Power

During the fourteenth century, Central Asia produced yet another aggressive empire builder—one who would revive the fortunes of the region and contribute enormously to its Islamic heritage. Born into a Turkicized Mongol tribe that had adopted Islam, the early career of Timur (r. 1369-1405), also known in the West as Tamerlane, was spent working in the services of pagan Mongol warriors.

Fired by his ambitions to control the lucrative East-West trade routes, Timur carved out a huge empire that at its peak stretched from Turkey to India. He transformed Samarkand, which had been mercilessly ravaged by Genghis Khan in the previous century, into one of the greatest cities the world had ever seen. He had a reputation for absolute ruthlessness that was worthy of Genghis Khan. Like Genghis, Timur had a penchant for building pyramids with the heads of the enemies he slaughtered. He committed countless massacres in the cities and towns he captured and looted and routinely ignored Muslim obligations regarding the safety of Christians.

Once again, however, Timur continued the paradoxical renaissance of the arts that took place after the violent invasions of the region. During his rule and that of his successors, known as the Timurids, architecture, literature, and the sciences flourished.

Timur's own grandson Ulugh Beg was one of the finest astronomers the world had seen, and oversaw the construction of a magnificent observatory in the capital. It was under the Timurids that the legendary fifteenth-century poet and statesman Ali Shir Nava'i thrived. One of Uzbekistan's best-known figures and a giant in the world of Persian literature, he also popularized the Turkish dialect of Chagatai, which now became a literary language in its own right.

Similarly, Timur brought a significant part of Afghanistan into the realm of his Muslim empire and the city of Herat (now in western Afghanistan) also became a flourishing cultural and scientific center.

Ibn Khaldun—Islam's Great Historian

One of Islam's greatest historians, Ibn Khaldun played a part in negotiating a treaty between the Mamluks and Timur and in so doing managed to meet one of the characters in the pages of his own book. Born in Tunis (in Tunisia) on May 27, 1332, Ibn Khaldun led a colorful and exciting life in the stormy politics of the Arabic world. His *Kitab al-Ibar* (*Universal History*) and its ground-breaking introduction, the *Muqaddima*, which forms a separate volume, rank amongst the finest academic works ever to be produced in the medieval world.

Ibn Khaldun was descended from a Spanish Arab family based in Seville that had come to North Africa as refugees fleeing the onslaught of the Christian reconquest of the Iberian Peninsula. As a young man, he worked in the courts of Tunis and Morocco. Eventually he sailed for Spain, where, in 1364, he led a Muslim mission to negotiate a peace treaty with the ruthless Castilian king, Pedro the Cruel.

His reward was an estate in Granada, the last Muslim kingdom in Spain, where he lived with his family. In the climate of the time, enemies were all too easy to make, and Ibn Khaldun was forced to abandon Granada for his personal safety. He spent the next few years restlessly traveling around North Africa and Spain, working in various posts including that of prime minister in Algeria.

Before long, concerns for his personal safety forced him to move further afield, and having arranged to make a pilgrimage to Mecca, he stopped en route in Cairo in 1382. He was greatly impressed by what he saw. Writing of the city's splendor and wealth he was moved to quote the words of a former teacher who had declared: "What one sees in dreams surpasses reality, but all that one could dream of Cairo falls short of the truth!"

For Ibn Khaldun, the Egyptian capital was also a wondrous oasis of learning. North Africa and Muslim Spain, he declared, had fallen into ruin, yet Egypt's thousands of years of unbroken tradition as a flourishing center of learning, in recent times reinforced by the Ayyubids and the Mamluks, served as a beacon that attracted students and scholars from Morocco to Iraq and beyond.

Ibn Khaldun (1332–1406), commemorated on a stamp from Tunisia, the land of his birth.

As was befitting of a man of his caliber, Ibn Khaldun began to teach at the famed Al-Azhar Mosque, while also finding time to continue writing. The Sultan Barquq, who had summoned Ibn Khaldun on his arrival, soon promoted him to the prestigious post of Grand Qadi (or Chief Justice) of the Malikites, one of the four legal schools of Sunnism. It was a job in which Ibn Khaldun distinguished himself, reforming and rooting out the corruption that was endemic in the legal system. The post exposed him to the intrigues of his enemies, however, and as a result, during his life he was forced to step down on no less than five occasions, only to be reelected each time.

Ibn Khaldun's life was struck by tragedy in 1384 after he had sent for his family to join him in Cairo. When their ship was wrecked approaching the port of Alexandria, they all drowned. Devastated, Ibn Khaldun yearned for a quieter life and, in 1387, he finally made the Hajj, the pilgrimage to Mecca. On his return, he was chosen to head Egypt's most important Sufi school. Yet before long, he was back in the limelight once again as Grand Qadi.

In 1400, his diplomatic skills were put to good use by the Mamluk government after Timur's major offensive westwards. After taking Baghdad, Timur marched on Damascus, in Mamluk Syria, and he lay siege to the city. Ibn Khaldun was one of a number of notables who were chosen to accompany Barquq's ten-year-old successor, Nasir Faraj, to Damascus in order to negotiate a treaty with Timur. Ibn Khaldun, who famously had to be lowered over the walls of the city by rope, played an important part in its subsequent surrender and it was at this time that he got to see the Great Khan. At the meeting, he took the opportunity to show Timur what he had written about him in his *Universal History*. The ruler was apparently so delighted that he offered his own suggestions and opinions.

It was first-hand experience such as this, combined with a good knowledge of history, that made Ibn Khaldun a unique chronicler. Yet it was his scientific approach to the subject, as demonstrated in his *Muqaddima* and *Universal History*, that sealed his reputation as an extraordinary figure in the Muslim world.

Begun in 1375, during a period of uncharacteristic seclusion in a castle in the present-day region of Algeria, the works bring together a wide variety of topics, including philosophy, religion, politics, economics, and even language to elaborate his theory of world history. When it came to geography, Ibn Khaldun's knowledge, like that of his Muslim contemporaries, was far superior to his European medieval counterparts.

His work, which he hoped might shed light on what factors contributed to the rise and fall of civilizations, has been hailed as the first comprehensive critical study of history, and one that predated modern sociology by hundreds of years. Ibn Khaldun's genius as a writer and teacher earned him enormous respect from his peers, and he is generally credited with reviving historical writing in Egypt. On March 17, 1406, while still in his sixth term as Grand Qadi, the great man died at at the age of seventy-four. As were his wishes, his body was laid to rest in a Sufi cemetery in Cairo.

Islam on the Periphery
—Travels in Africa and Asia

"In every Chinese city there is a quarter for Muslims in which they live by themselves, and in which they have mosques both for the Friday services and for other religious purposes . . . the Muslims are honored and respected."
—Ibn Battuta, Travels *(1355)*

The Journeys of Ibn Battuta

By the fourteenth century, the Islamic world had suffered major setbacks, and it would be some time until new empires would bring it back into the international limelight. Yet on another level, the Islamic world was alive and well and enjoying the fruits of the international trade system it had established over the past centuries.

A man who witnessed this world firsthand was Ibn Battuta, a traveling Islamic scholar and judge, and considered by many to be "the world's first tourist." A contemporary of Marco Polo, his travels were astonishing not only because of the huge distances—perhaps some 75,000 miles in some thirty years, making him the most traveled person known in the medieval world—and the numerous hazards he survived, but also because they served to illustrate the interconnectedness of the world in which he lived.

Not only could Ibn Battuta benefit from the routes paved by many generations of pilgrims to Mecca, but also from the extensive caravan and sea routes throughout Africa, Asia, and the Indian Ocean that were dominated by Muslim merchants. Even in the lands that were not directly ruled by Muslims, he was able to find settled and flourishing Muslim communities that welcomed him as one of their own.

Resolving never, if possible, to cover any road a second time and mixing with emperors, mystics, merchants, and beggars alike, his writings abound with fascinating tales and observations of life in the fourteenth century. Today he is still considered a primary source of medieval geography as well as an authority on Islamic culture and society.

Of Berber origins, Ibn Battuta was born in Tangier, Morocco, on February 24, 1304, into a family that had produced several *qadis* or Islamic judges. In June 1325, at the age of twenty-one, he set out on his very first journey. Dictating his memoirs, he recounted:

> I left Tangier, my birthplace, with the intention of making the Pilgrimage to the Holy House and the tomb of the Prophet [i.e. Mecca and Medina]. I set out alone, finding no companion to cheer the way with friendly conversation, and no travelers to accompany me. Driven by an overwhelming impulse within me, and a long-cherished desire to visit those glorious sanctuaries, I resolved to quit all my friends and tear myself away from my home. As my parents were still alive, it weighed grievously upon me to part from them, and both they and I were afflicted with sorrow.

The inspiration for his travels is not at all surprising. The obligation of every Muslim to make the Hajj at least once in their lifetime, if it lies in his or her power to do so, is one that throughout the ages has provided a powerful stimulus to travel.

Despite his admission of feeling alone at the outset of the journey, he was following a path well-trodden by so many others. Though the journey to Mecca was hazardous, pilgrims traveled in organized caravans, often under armed guard if conditions proved exceptionally dangerous, and made scheduled stops along the way. Long-established religious charities provided for the pilgrims' needs at principal rest stops and caravanserais along the way.

The route from Cairo to Aydhab, not so far from the major port of Aden on the Red Sea, proved too dangerous on account of bandits, and Ibn Battuta was forced to turn back, taking the alternative land route via Gaza and Jerusalem, before finally reaching Mecca in October 1326.

The Holy City of Islam bustled with the countless pilgrims who had arrived from all parts of the Islamic world, and, as was befitting the great spiritual center of Islam, it also thronged with eminent religious scholars. The sense of community Ibn Battuta found there greatly impressed him:

> The inhabitants of Mecca are distinguished by many excellent and noble activities and qualities, by their beneficence to the humble and weak, and by their kindness to strangers. When any of them makes a feast, he begins by giving food to the religious devotees who are poor and without resources, inviting them first with kindness and delicacy.

The young traveler found the experience of mixing with fellow-Muslims from far-off lands exhilarating, fueling a passion to continue traveling that would draw him to a life on the move, taking him to East and West Africa, Spain, the steppes of southern Russia, Siberia, Persia, Central Asia, India, Sri Lanka, the Maldives, China, and Indonesia.

In East Africa

Ibn Battuta reached the coast of East Africa in 1331. There, Muslim communities had already been long established. Over the course of several centuries Muslim traders—in search of gold, ivory, ingredients with which to make perfumes, and slaves—had settled in increasing numbers in the major ports along the Indian Ocean. Their activities helped to push the influence of Islam ever further south, along the coastal towns of East Africa, where by the end of the tenth century it had reached Mombasa, Mozambique, and the spice island of Zanzibar.

Ibn Battuta's stepping stone into East Africa was the port of Aden in Yemen, the linchpin in international trade in the Indian Ocean. He called it "the port of the Indians," visited by "large vessels from Calicut, Kinbyat [Cambay], Kawlam [Quilon] . . . and many other Malabar ports." The Indian port of Calicut mentioned here was another vital link in the trade chain "visited by men from China, Sumatra, Ceylon, the Maldives, Yemen, and Fars, and in it gather merchants from all quarters."

Ibn Battuta marveled at the wealth of the Egyptians, Indians, and other traders of Aden who were "so rich that sometimes a single merchant is the sole owner of a large ship with all it contains." And often the ships could carry a considerable amount. The main sailing

Swahili—A World Language Forged by Trade

The development of the Swahili language is inextricably linked to Islam. During the tenth century, Muslim traders from the Red Sea began to control trade routes along the east coast of Africa, which with its annual cycle of trade winds or monsoons had long been a vital part of a much larger network of interregional trade stretching to the other side of the Indian Ocean and on to China, as well as to the Mediterranean.

With the growing trade, Muslims settled in increasing numbers in the coastal villages and towns, many marrying into local populations. Although African languages continued to be spoken, a trade language known as Swahili (from the Arabic word for "Coast Lands") developed. Based on the structure of Bantu, a dominant language group in the region, Swahili absorbed numerous terms and concepts from Arabic and Persian.

As trade spread, so too did the language, although it remained largely a coastal phenomenon. Interaction with the peoples living within the region of the Indian Ocean saw Swahili spread to places such as the islands of Comoros and Madagascar, and further to Oman, the United Arab Emirates, and to South Africa. Today it is the most widespread African language spoken on the continent—by people of all creeds.

vessels that plied the trade routes were called dhows, and the larger ones could have as many as thirty crew members.

Following the very same routes and voyaging on similar vessels, Ibn Battuta was able to visit the key ports of the East African Coast. Among the first was Zeila, which lay within the Christian kingdom of Ethiopia, but which had a large community of Muslim traders. He described it as:

> . . . a large city with a great bazaar, but which is the dirtiest, most abominable, and most stinking town in the world. The reason for the stench is the quantity of its fish and the blood of the camels that they slaughter in the streets. When we got there we chose to spend the night at sea, in spite of its extreme roughness, rather than in the town, because of its filth.

Further down the coast at Mogadishu, a bustling and wealthy port (today the capital of Somalia) where Arabic and Persian were spoken everywhere, Ibn Battuta was taken to meet the Sultan, because, as he was informed on arriving, "it is the custom that whenever a theologian, or *sharif* ("descendant of the Prophet"), or a man of religion comes here, he must see the Sultan before taking his lodging."

Below Mogadishu lay the territories of the Swahili people, a name that derives from *As-Sawahil* or "Coast Lands," the Arabic name for the part of the coast that stretches along present-day Kenya and Tanzania. In Mombasa (today in Kenya), Ibn Battuta witnessed the well-built wooden mosques that Muslims had constructed to worship in. In the major trading port of Kilwa—"a very fine and substantially built town" characterized by wooden houses—Muslim merchants had successfully cornered a great deal of the Indian Ocean trade, which included items such as gold, silver, pearls, perfumes, crockery from Arabia, earthenware from Persia, and porcelain from China.

Ibn Battuta reported that the Sultan of Kilwa regularly organized expeditions into the interior of East Africa to seize slaves and other prizes, and that "he devoted the fifth part of the booty made on his expeditions to pious and charitable purposes, as prescribed in the Qur'an." Ibn Battuta was happy to note that the Sultan had the greatest of respect for religious scholars as well as men of noble descent.

In West Africa

Meanwhile, in West Africa, over on the other side of the continent, it was caravan rather than sea routes that had helped to bring Islam into the region. Stimulated by the bustling economic activity in North Africa, trade across the great desert wastes of the Sahara had seen significant parts of West Africa come into contact with Muslim merchants. Great trade centers emerged on the major caravan routes such as Koumbi Saleh in Mali and Timbuktu, where African slaves, ivory, ostrich feathers, and especially gold were exchanged for salt, cloth, glass, ceramics, and other luxuries from the north.

Not surprisingly, Ibn Battuta followed the very same routes, setting out from the Moroccan city of Fez in the fall of 1354. Although a camel train heading from the Mediterranean Coast for West Africa, via the inhospitable Sahara Desert, may have seemed a huge undertaking in the fourteenth century, the bonds of religion and trade were powerful enough to make light of great distances. En route, Ibn Battuta stopped at Sijilmasa, on the Moroccan side of the desert, where he met and stayed with the "learned Abu Muhammad al-Bushri, the man whose brother I met in the city of Qanjanfu in China." Even for a man as well-

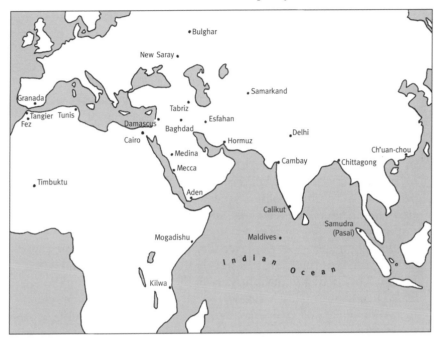

Ibn Battuta's world—some of the cities visited by the wandering judge that were either under Islamic rule or had well-established Muslim communites.

traveled as himself who was always chancing upon acquaintances, Ibn Battuta was somewhat amazed and commented: "How strangely separated they are!"

By the time Ibn Battuta had set foot in the region, the rulers of Mali had already converted to Islam. Only two years before Ibn Battuta's first visit to Cairo in 1326, the ruler of Mali, Mansa (or "Sultan") Musa (*d.* 1337) had passed through the streets of the very same city, accompanied by a huge retinue and camels laden with riches en route to Mecca. He spent so much gold in Cairo that it led to a devaluation of the precious metal in the Egyptian economy.

Once in Mali, Ibn Battuta met with the ruling Sultan Sulayman. Ibn Battuta had expected that a scholar and judge of his pedigree, who had worked in the courts of other rulers, could expect a generous gift from the Sultan, especially since the previous rulers of Mali had a reputation for great generosity. He was wrong, and instead of the "robes of honor and money" he anticipated, he merely received "three cakes of bread, a piece of beef fried in native oil, and a calabash of sour curds." Only by complaining directly to Sulayman did he get substantially more:

> I have traveled through the countries of the world and have met their kings. Yet I have already been here for four months and you have neither shown me hospitality, nor given me anything. What am I to say about you in front of other rulers?

In the cities at least, there were clear indications that the rites of Islam were taken seriously. In Mali, for example, Ibn Battuta observed that people were "careful to observe the hours of prayer, and assiduous in attending them in congregations, and in bringing up their children to respect them."

On his itinerary was the legendary city of Timbuktu, which was just beginning to blossom as a hugely important commercial nexus. Founded by Tuareg nomads at start of the twelfth century (although little is known of its early history), Timbuktu would become one of the major centers of the lucrative trans-Saharan trade network.

Annexed by Mansa Musa in 1325, the commercial center was also to become a major focus for Muslim scholarship. In Timbuktu, noted Ibn Battuta, "is the grave of the meritorious poet Al-Sahali, from Granada." In fact the Spaniard was more than a poet, he was also the architect of the impressive main mosque in Timbuktu. Al-Sahali had met Mansa Musa in Mecca while making the pilgrimage and was persuaded to accompany the Sultan back to Mali. The mosque, which is shaped like a pyramid at its base and features conical towers, had its own university that became renowned for its brilliance, attracting academics and students from afar.

Stamp commemorating Ibn Battutua.

After its incorporation into the West African Songhai Empire, which peaked in the fifteenth and sixteenth centuries, Timbuku enjoyed a period of unprecedented prosperity, despite the odd setback. As a center of learning, the city's reputation was unrivaled in the region. In the mid-sixteenth century it boasted approximately 150 Islamic schools, with students flooding in from North Africa and the Middle East. According to Leon the African, a historian of the period, in the markets of Songhai learned books were always in great demand, and in Timbuktu the wealth of traders could be measured by the number of manuscripts in their libraries.

In Southeast Asia

Ibn Battuta also lived and worked for a number of years in the Islamic Sultanate of Delhi, in northern India. When he was chosen by the Sultan of India to be his ambassador to the ruler of China, the indefatigable *qadi* headed off on another remarkable journey, stopping off en route in the islands of the Maldives, Ceylon, the deltas of Bengal, and Indonesia.

Islam was already firmly established in the Maldives, and Ibn Battuta noted with satisfaction that all its inhabitants were Muslim. However, he remarked on their timidity, describing how some fainted when, in his role as a judge, he ordered a thief's hand to be cut off.

In 1345, he arrived by a Chinese junk on the shores of the island of Sumatra. Islam had begun to establish a firm presence in Malaysia and Indonesia during the thirteenth century with the creation of the Muslim port city-states, most of them trading centers, the earliest of which was Pasai in north Sumatra, although Muslim Arab and Indian merchants had been active in the region long before.

Trade was a great incentive for rulers to convert to Islam, and many did so. It enabled them to participate in the large trade networks of the Muslim world. Muslim traders found themselves welcome in the city-states, as did educated Muslims such as Ibn Battuta, who were encouraged to settle and take administrative, judicial, and religious posts.

The city of Pasai was, according to Ibn Battuta, "a large and beautiful city encompassed by a wooden wall with wooden towers." The Sultan he described as "a most illustrious and open-handed ruler, and a lover of theologians. He is constantly engaged in warring for the Faith [against the infidels] and in raiding expeditions, but is a humble-hearted man, who walks on foot to the Friday prayers." As with other

Muslim-controlled lands, non-Muslims living in the vicinity were expected to pay the special *jizya* poll tax.

Despite Ibn Battuta's account of the Sultan's raiding expeditions, Islam was not spread in an aggressive manner in the region. There were no zealous priests, nor was there a concerted effort to stamp out traditional animist beliefs, and these continued to thrive. Only very gradually would Islam begin to gain ground outside the city-states. The key players helping its spread were Sufis, whose mysticism and non-dogmatic approach did not clash with local religious sensitivities, and allowed for a looser interpretation of their newfound faith.

Eventually, the majority of the population across Indonesia and Malaysia would come to adopt Islam, although the local traditions and cultures continued to exert an enormous influence. To this day, Islam in the region is imbued with a distinctive Southeast Asian character, aided by the fact that while religious courts existed everywhere in Muslim society, Islamic law was permitted to blend on certain levels with the region's traditional legal code, called "adat."

In China

Ibn Battuta soon made his way on to China to fulfill his mission. A Muslim presence had been established in the land from as early as the seventh century via the trade sea routes in the southeast and the great Silk Road land route in the west. Numerous cities along these routes gradually became home to flourishing communities of Muslim merchants from a variety of ethnic backgrounds, including Arabs, Persians, and Mongols.

The sea routes were an exciting area of expansion at the time of Ibn Battuta. They provided an alternative to the fabled Silk Road itself, where the dangers of travel were increased by roving armies, bandits, and unpredictable governments. Each small kingdom along the Silk Road routes taxed merchants along the way, making their goods more expensive to the end buyer. While none of this lessened demand for such merchandise, it nevertheless pushed traders into searching for other ways to transport their wares.

Although merchant ships had always traveled the seaways between China and the Middle East, the unpredictability of the land routes, combined with improvements in shipbuilding and navigation, increasingly provided merchants with the reasons they needed to sell their camels and invest in ships. Sailing ships also had the advantage of being faster than camel caravans and could carry far more cargo per journey. Goods went from east to west, west to east, from Spain to China and back according to demand. To China went grapes, wine, alfalfa, cucumbers, figs, pomegranates, sesame, chives, coriander, saffron, domesticated horses, and bactrian camels, along with the principles of astronomy, and medicine. From China came silk, roses, azaleas, chrysanthemums, peonies, camellias, gunpowder, paper, printing, and armor. Cinnamon came from the East African Coast, while cloves, nutmeg, and ginger were exported from the Spice Islands (today's Indonesia), where the Javanese brought rice; the Chinese brought porcelains, as well as coins, brass gongs, and cloth; the Indians brought cotton, silk, beads—all bartered for local spices, tree resins, bird of paradise plumes, and sea slugs, considered by many to be a great delicacy.

A typical trading center was Canton (modern-day Guangzhou), described by Ibn Battuta as:

> . . . a city of first rank in regard to the size and quality of its bazaars. One of the largest of those is the porcelain bazaar, from which porcelain is exported to all parts of China, to India, and to Yemen. Silk is used for clothing even by poor monks and beggars. Its porcelains are the finest of all makes of pottery and its hens are bigger than geese in our country.

The rulers of China at the time of Ibn Batutta's visit were the powerful descendants of Genghis Khan and the Mongol Dynasty, known as the Yuan Dynasty (1260-1368). Although not Muslims, they welcomed Muslim traders into China during this period, and the Emperor himself recruited foreigners as advisers to his administration.

Muslims, and even a few Europeans such as Marco Polo, held jobs in China as tax-collectors, architects, and finance officers. The rulers had an "open door" policy which was geared to actively encouraging trade abroad. And so Muslim merchants were welcomed into the southern Chinese cities, especially Zaytun (modern-day Quanzhou) and Canton on the southern coast. The incomers generally lived in their own neighborhoods, where they built mosques, hospitals, and

Schematic depiction of the world, typical of medieval maps. This dates from fourteenth-century Baghdad and shows the world surrounded by water—the lower semicircle represents the Mediterranean Sea while the higher represents the Red Sea.

bazaars, and conducted trade by shipping routes that extended all the way back to the Persian Gulf, Red Sea, and Indian Ocean ports.

Muslim travelers such as Ibn Battuta knew that they could always find Muslim hospitality in the major sea ports. The Prophet Muhammad had even encouraged travel and learning in the Far East in one of his sayings: "Seek knowledge, even as far as China." Ibn Battuta mentioned the ease and safety with which he was able to travel in China, a place where "a man may go by himself on a nine-months' journey, carrying with him large sums of money, without any fear on that account." Muslims entering a city were given the choice of staying with a named merchant within the Muslim community or going to a "hostelry." Cities would also have a *Shaykh al-Islam* ("Spiritual Leader"), who would act as an intermediary between the Muslim community and the government, and a *qadi* to oversee matters relating to local Muslim laws.

Ibn Battuta described how merchants living the city of Zaytun were happy to honor the spirit of the Qur'an by giving alms to the wayfarer. Always overjoyed to meet new Muslim arrivals, "they declare 'He has come from the land of Islam!' and make the new arrival the recipient of tithes on their properties, so that he becomes as rich as themselves."

But it was all a little too perfect for Ibn Battuta's taste:

China was beautiful, but it did not please me. On the contrary, I was greatly troubled thinking about the way paganism dominated this country. Whenever I went out of my lodging, I saw many blameworthy things. That disturbed me so much that I stayed indoors most of the time and only went out when necessary. During my stay in China, whenever I saw any Muslims I always felt as though I were meeting my own family and close kinsmen.

Ibn Battuta's incredible journeys clearly highlight the extent of Islam's reach, vividly illustrating that fact that with a home in every port and every caravanserai, the Islamic world was truly at the center of a three-continent system of commerce that Europe could so far only dream of. The monopoly was such that, when the Portuguese explorer and trader Vasco de Gama was asked in 1498, what his country was looking for, he replied in frustration from his ship in Calicut: "Spices . . . and Christians to trade with!"

The Taj Mahal Mausoleum in Agra, India.

The Age of the Three Great Muslim Empires

Ottoman *sepahi* (cavalryman) from the sixteenth century.

The Ottomans

*"Despite real defects in governance and periods of civil disorder, the Empire
continued its tolerance of diversity until enemies, internal and external,
destroyed it. It is not the heritage of Ottoman rule that has been
seen in modern ethnic and religious conflict in the
Middle East and the Balkans."*
—*Justin McCarthy* (The Ottoman Peoples and the End of Empire)

By the fifteenth century, the Muslim world had long seemed to
have lost its way, and dreams of a politically united, greater
Islamic community seemed further away than ever. External
assaults by enemies, such as the Christians and Mongols, and internal
conflicts had taken their toll. Attempting to match religious unity
with political unity had been problematic from the start, and became
increasingly more so as Islam extended its reach ever further and over
more diversified populations. The once hopeful institution of the
Caliphate had crumbled along with Baghdad, now only surviving in a
toothless and limited form in Egypt thanks to the Mamluks whose
purpose it served.

Yet in the fifteenth and sixteenth centuries there would be a
dramatic shift in the fortunes of the Muslim world, with the rise of the
great empires of the Ottomans, Safavids, and Mughals, centered in
Turkey, Iran, and India, respectively. Each of these was ruled by a
dynasty with direct Turkic connections yet with very different
interpretations of Islam. Each was also responsible for outstanding
achievements, enjoying their respective Golden Ages and leaving
their indelible signatures on world history.

Rise of the Ottoman Empire

The immense empire of the Ottomans, established on the ruins of the
once-great Eastern Roman Empire of Byzantium, would prove to be
the powerbroker over half of the Mediterranean. Defenders of
"orthodox" Sunnism, for much of their history the Ottomans

constituted Western Europe's greatest rival, one that pushed the boundaries of Islam firmly into southeastern Europe, and nearly into the heartland of Europe itself.

The founders of the Ottoman Empire were members of that ubiquitous group of peoples, the Turks. As we have seen, the waves of nomadic Turkic tribes entering the region of the Middle East from Central Asia had a great impact on the Middle East. It was the Seljuk

Hagia Sofia, once the greatest cathedral in Christendom, was converted into a mosque after the Ottomans captured Constantinople. In the twentieth century it became a museum.

Turks who seized power in Baghdad in the eleventh century and reduced the Abbasid Caliphs there to figureheads.

The Seljuk Sultanate of Rum, comprising the eastern part of Anatolia, had been hit hard by the Mongol attacks, and so it broke up into a number of petty states. Living on the frontiers of the Byzantine Empire, these Turks were highly militant and launched continual raids into Christian territories, inspired by the notion of jihad.

Under their energetic leader Osman (after whom the Ottomans, or "Osmanlis," are named), they were able in 1326 to seize the important Byzantine city of Bursa, which lay some fifty miles south of Constantinople. The city became the new power center from which they were able to continue their expansion, eventually invading southeast Europe, skirting around the Byzantine capital. There, Osman's descendant Sultan Murad headed a huge army that defeated a combined force of Serb, Bulgar, and Croat forces in 1389 at the historic battle of Kosovo. In so doing, the Ottomans brought the Balkans squarely under their control—and, once again, Islam had a firm foothold in Europe.

Surrounded by the Ottoman forces, Constantinople inevitably fell in 1453. The event brought the final curtain down on a thousand years of Byzantine history. What once had been the greatest city in Christendom was renamed Istanbul (the common popular name for the city), in order to remove reference to the first Holy Roman Emperor Constantine, after whom it had been named. From now on it would again take its place on the world stage, this time as the capital of the great Ottoman Empire.

The Ottomans also adopted the legendary Hagia Sofia Cathedral, which in its present form dates from the sixth century. Built for Justinian, Emperor of Eastern Rome (of which Constantinople was also the capital), its soaring domes once made it the greatest cathedral in Christendom. It was sacked by the Crusaders but the Ottomans treated the building with great respect and turned it into a mosque—four minarets were added at a later date. However, in keeping with Muslim religious beliefs, images of the holy family and other sacred figures were painted over, and other Christian symbols removed from sight.

The capture of Constantinople prompted the city's cardinal to lament to the Doge of Venice that:

> . . . it was a terrible thing to relate and to be deplored by all who have in them any spark of humanity, and especially by Christians. Much danger threatens Italy, not to mention other lands, if the violent assaults of the most ferocious barbarians are not checked.

He had not overestimated the power of the Ottomans. They went on to amass a vast collection of territories that not only included a sizeable part of the Middle East and Northern Africa, but also substantial parts of southeastern Europe, including Greece, Bosnia, Serbia, Albania, Bulgaria, and Moldova.

The conquest of the Mamluks in Egypt by Selim the Grim in 1516 and 1517 proved to be highly significant. Not only did the Ottomans capture Egypt, a rich source of taxes and a major producer of grain, rice, and sugar, but they also gained control over the two holiest cities of Islam—Mecca and Medina. Echoing the Mamluks before them, who once had brought the Abbasid Caliph from Baghdad, Selim now had the Caliph in Egypt, Mutawakkil, himself a descendant of the Abbasids, brought to Istanbul. He also carried off a casket of holy relics consisting of Muhammad's mantle and military banner, and had them placed in the great Topkapi Palace.

The Ottomans themselves had pretensions to the Caliphate, and claimed among their many grand titles to be Caliphs of the Muslim world. Selim himself was styled the "Caliph of God throughout the length and breadth of the earth." These were lofty claims, yet it was not until much later that this would be seriously taken to imply that they had a "legal right" to the position as understood during the era of the Abbasid Caliphs in Baghdad.

Sultans such as Suleyman the Magnificent (*r.* 1520-1566) were keen to be seen as playing an active role as defenders of Islam, protecting Muslim interests around the world. In 1538 he dispatched a fleet to oust the Portuguese from the island of Diu in India, sent technical aid to help the Sultan of Aceh in Sumatra, and planned an expedition to expel the Muscovites from the Lower Volga to free trade and pilgrimage routes for the Muslims in Central Asia.

It was ironic that despite the Ottomans' desire to promote Muslim unity in the world, for more than two centuries they would engage in near continual military campaigns against their fellow Muslim neighbors in the Persian Empire, whose ruling Safavid dynasty were staunch defenders of the Shi'i rite. It proved to be a costly and fruitless exercise in which frontier territories, especially in the region of the Caucasus, would find themselves passed back and forth in a succession of failed treaties.

Under Selim, the elite troops known as the Janissaries came into their element as the linchpin of the Sultan's might. The Janissaries (from the Turkish *yeniçeri* meaning "new soldier" or "trooper") were a highly disciplined and effective fighting force that had been established in the early days of the empire. Their ranks comprised Christian youths recruited from the empire, who, having converted to Islam, were then subjected to rigorous military training. Their reward was a life of privilege. However, as they grew in strength and influence, they eventually became a somewhat troublesome force, and regularly involved themselves in palace plots and coups. By the eighteenth century, entry restrictions were relaxed to allow entry to Muslim youths while laws were lifted that prevented Janissaries from marrying, with the result that sons often followed in the footsteps of their fathers.

Meanwhile, trade bustled under the protection of the Ottomans. A ceaseless flow of goods made its way along the great caravan routes of the empire, laden on camels or in ox-drawn carts. Major caravan routes ran from Istanbul to Cairo, via Aleppo in Syria. From Istanbul caravans also headed out east to Iran, via Erzurum and Diyarbakir, as well as west to Belgrade in Europe. Cairo was a major interchange, with routes leading out to Morocco and a pilgrim caravan to Mecca that was protected by tribesmen under the pay of the Ottomans.

Non-Muslim Populations under the Ottomans

The Ottomans installed Sharia law in their empire, which gave a good deal of power to the religious establishment. Yet the Ottoman Empire was noted for its tolerant attitude towards non-Muslims living under its jurisdiction. Immediately after the Ottomans took over Constantinople, Isaac Zarfati, a Jew living in the city, asked his fellow Jews of the Rhineland to consider:

> Is it not better for you to live under Muslims than under Christians? Here every man may dwell at peace under his own vine and his own fig tree. In Christendom on the contrary, ye dare not even venture to clothe your children in red or blue according to your taste without exposing them to insult and yourself to extortion; and therefore are ye not condemned to go about meanly clad in sad-colored rainment?

In the Asiatic provinces the Ottoman population was mainly Muslim (Turks, Arabs, and Kurds mostly), yet there were also substantial Orthodox Christian (Armenians, Georgians, Assyrians, and Greeks) and Jewish populations. Anatolia itself (the land mass that corresponds to present-day Turkey), once predominantly Christian,

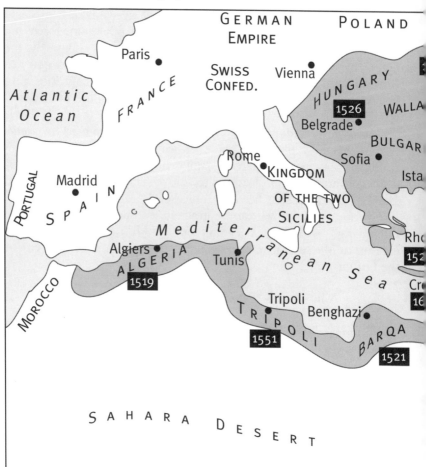

The Ottoman Empire & its Tributary States

in the Sixteenth & Seventeenth Centuries

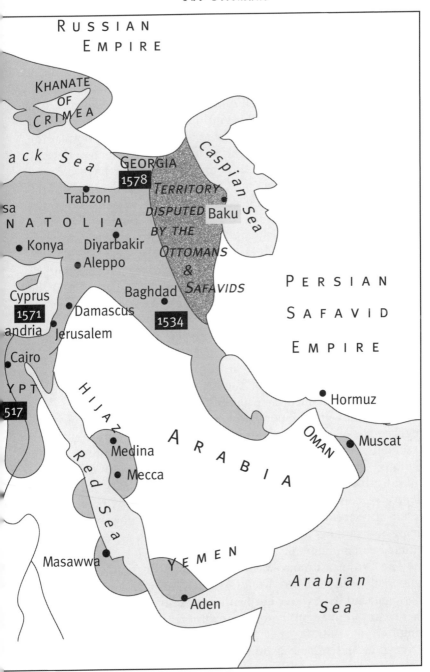

RUSSIAN
EMPIRE

KHANATE
OF
CRIMEA

ack Sea

GEORGIA
1578

Caspian Sea

TERRITORY
DISPUTED Baku
BY THE
OTTOMANS
&
SAFAVIDS

sa
NATOLIA
Trabzon

Konya   Diyarbakir
•Aleppo

Cyprus
1571
andria   Jerusalem
Damascus

Baghdad
1534

PERSIAN

SAFAVID

EMPIRE

Cairo
YPT
517

HIJAZ

Red Sea

ARABIA

Medina
Mecca

Hormuz

OMAN   Muscat

Masawwa

YEMEN

Aden

Arabian

Sea

had witnessed large-scale conversion to Islam early on, thanks to the efforts of militant Sufi orders as well as increasing numbers of Turks and other Muslims entering the region.

Meanwhile, Ottoman territories in southeastern Europe were predominantly Christian (Greeks, Bulgarians, Serbs, Montenegrins, and Vlahs) but also with significant Muslim minorities. Bosnia had been annexed by Sultan Bayezid II in 1463, who had little difficulty in encouraging the large heretical Slavic Christian sect in Bosnia, the Bogumils, to convert to Islam. The Serbians on the other hand largely remained Orthodox Christian, although their able warriors were used as a military buffer to protect the Ottoman northern flank against the Austrians. Their role as mercenaries in wars waged against the Habsburg Empire intensified the traditional animosity between Orthodox Chrisitian Serbians and Catholic Austrians. The Croats on the other hand remained essentially Catholic, and were never absorbed by the Ottoman Empire. By the end of the fifteenth century, Croatia was annexed to the Habsburg Empire, and its role as the southernmost protector of the Austrian Empire was reinforced by the Habsburg troops.

Ottoman domination in Eastern Europe and the Balkans left a lasting left a lasting legacy of Islam in the region and today there are significant Muslim populations in Albania, Bulgaria, Romania, and Bosnia. The latter was part of Yugoslavia, whose breakup during the 1990s led to a sustained campaign of persecution of Muslims.

Community life of non-Muslims in the Ottoman Empire was regulated by what became known as the millet system. The millets, or "religious communities," had their own leaders appointed by the Sultan. Under the arrangement minorities were afforded a considerable range of religious and cultural freedom, and a good degree of control over administrative, tax, and legal matters. As a result of reciprocal arrangements with European powers, foreigners living and working in the Ottoman territory, such as Catholics, were granted certain immunity from Ottoman laws.

The Ottoman Empire was also a major destination for many Jews who had been expelled from Western Europe, including Spain, Portugal, and Italy, where during the sixteenth century the authorities had begun to mete out highly repressive treatment. In the Ottoman Empire, in contrast, they found themselves welcome—afforded protection and what constituted a package of basic human rights.

Such conditions allowed outcast Jewish communities to regroup and flourish and play a highly active role in the Ottoman economy. During the sixteenth century, Jews helped to turn certain Ottoman ports, especially Salonica in Greece, into major international trade centers that rivaled Venice. A number of Jews attained positions of great importance, becoming dukes and ambassadors. Illustrious Jewish families also came to play a hugely influential role in the Empire's banking and financial world.

Sinan—Architect of the Sultans

A visit to Istanbul today testifies to the greatness of Ottoman architecture. Among the finest works are those drafted by the hand of Mimar Sinan, regarded by many as one of the greatest architects in the Islamic world. Sinan (*c.* 1489-1588) was born in a village near Kayseri, central Anatolia, to an Orthodox Christian family. He entered his father's trade as a stone mason and carpenter, but was drafted into the Janissary corps where he followed a career as a construction officer. It was not long before his architectural talents began to reveal themselves and, progressing from constructing bridges and fortifications, he eventually began to work on non-military buildings. Holding the prestigious post of Royal Architect, Sinan was responsible for more than three hundred buildings, including scores of fine mosques, in the Ottoman Empire.

Sinan's best-known work is the outstanding Suleymaniye Mosque in Istanbul, built for Suleyman the Magnificent. With its four towering yet fragile minarets and its great dome, the mosque imparts an aura of near-magic in its setting overlooking the Golden Horn, an inlet of the Bosphorus.

While Sinan considered the Suleymaniye Mosque to be his work of "maturity," he considered his masterpiece to be the Selimiye Mosque in Edirne, built when he was in his eighties. He wrote:

> Christians say they have defeated the Muslims because no dome has been built in the Islamic world which can rival the dome of the Hagia Sofia. It greatly grieved my heart that they should say that to build so large a dome was so difficult a task. I determined to erect such a mosque, and with the help of God, in the reign of Sultan Selim Khan, I made the

dome of this mosque six cubits wider and four cubits [one cubit is approximately 18 inches] deeper than the dome of the Hagia Sofia.

Suleyman the Magnificent Builds his Empire

On a military front, after the victorious assault on Constantinople in 1453, successive Ottoman rulers gained lands in the central and northern Balkans to add to their holdings of Turkey, Greece, Serbia, and Bulgaria. In addition, northern Africa stretching from Algeria to Egypt, the eastern Mediterranean countries of Syria, Palestine, and Jordan, and the entire Anatolian Peninsula to the east of the Bosphorus Straits were within the Ottoman orbit.

The man who made all this possible was the great Sultan Suleyman. Born in 1494 in Trabzon on the Black Sea coast, he ruled the Empire for forty-six years between 1520-1566. The Europeans called him the "Magnificent"—not without some envy—but the Ottomans called him "Kanuni" or the "Lawgiver," and within the Empire he was responsible for dramatically transforming the army and the judicial system. Suleyman himself was a poet and accomplished goldsmith.

This was the Age of Discovery and Enlightenment, an exciting time for visionary reconstruction and grand city planning right across Europe, and Istanbul was no exception. Suleyman had a detailed urban plan for regeneration throughout his lengthy reign in which migration of the local populace and building houses around the city wall were prohibited. Coffeehouses were introduced to Istanbul during this period, an idea which was rapidly taken up in Europe. The port of Golden Horn, of which the surveillance was made from Galata Tower, became one of the busiest ports in the world.

The Empire had by now become known in Europe as "the Sublime Porte"—taken from the French, meaning the "lofty gate." The ancient city walls of Istanbul had twelve gates, and near one of these gates stood the apparatus of imperial power: the grand vizier's offices and those of all the chief ministers of state.

Western historians know Suleyman primarily as a conqueror. His military feats made him more feared in Europe than any other Islamic ruler before him. The Emperor was only too happy to exploit his reputation:

Istanbul's Suleymaniye Mosque was built by the royal architect Sinan and completed in 1557.

Slave of God, master of the world, I am Suleyman and my name is read in all the prayers in all the cities of Islam. I am the Shah of Baghdad and Iraq, Caesar of all the lands of Rome, and the Sultan of Egypt. I seized the Hungarian crown and gave it to the least of my slaves!

Even though he may not have occupied the entire extent of the "Roman" lands, he still claimed them as his own and almost launched an invasion of Rome itself (the city came within a hairbreadth of Ottoman invasion during Suleyman's expedition against Corfu).

At the Battle of Mohacs in 1526, the combined forces of the Hungarians, Wallachians, and Moldavans fell to Suleyman's army. Territories that comprised Romania and Hungary were added to the Ottoman Empire. Additionally, the Sultan's fleet had mastery of the Red Sea (including Yemen and Aden) and virtually the whole of the Mediterranean, waging war on the coasts of North Africa, Italy, and Dalmatia under the command of its fearsome admiral Barbarossa.

In 1529, Suleyman caused panic in Europe after his troops marched all the way to Vienna, the center of the powerful European

Habsburg dynasty. Laying siege to the city, the Ottomans seemed for a moment poised to march into the European heartland, but the venture was curtailed by adverse weather conditions. Shock waves rippled through Western Europe, which at the time was creaking under the strain of disputes and wars between Catholics and Protestants. The venture seriously undermined Christian unity and the security of the Holy Roman Empire. Nevertheless, the ultimate failure of the Ottomans to secure Vienna marked the first significant Turkish defeat and fixed the northern boundaries of the Empire near Vienna.

Besides his invasions and campaigns, Suleyman was a dynamic player in the politics of Europe. Just as the Europeans plotted against him, he too pursued an aggressive policy of European destabilization. His particular target was both the Roman Catholic church and the Holy Roman Empire, the alliance of Europe's Catholic countries bound by the Pope's spiritual authority. With the arrival of the Protestant Reformation—on the surface a religious phenomenon but in reality a series of powerful political and nationalist movements—

Suleyman I (also known as the "Magnificent") ruled over the Ottoman Empire from 1520-66.

the Holy Roman Empire started to break up, becoming fractured into Catholic and Protestant states. Suleyman's response was immediate: he poured financial support into the newly emerging Protestant countries in a bid to ensure that Europe remained religiously and politically divided and so ripe for an invasion. Many have since argued that Protestantism would never have succeeded in establishing itself if the Ottoman Empire had not provided it with financial backing.

It was more than an aggressive desire for territory that fueled Suleyman's policies—there was also a defensive element. Like most other non-Europeans, he fully understood the consequences of rapid Europe expansion that had been taking place, seeing in it a major threat to the Islamic world. Portugal had invaded several Muslim cities in eastern Africa in order to dominate trade with India, while the Russians were pushing Central Asians south as part of a policy of expansion. Accordingly, in addition to invading and destabilizing Europe, Suleyman also made it Ottoman policy to help any Muslim country threatened by European expansion. It was this role that gave him the right, in the eyes of the Ottomans, to declare himself supreme Caliph of Islam.

Troubled Years

Maintaining Suleyman's vigorous and successful foreign policy, would ultimately prove impossible. Dents in the image of Ottoman invincibility had begun to appear by the late sixteenth century. In an attempt to prevent the Ottomans from advancing up the Adriatic, a number of Christian states were able to overcome their mutual distrust and present a united front at the Battle of Lepanto in 1571. The showdown proved to be the

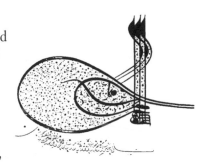

The tughra of Sultan Suleyman the Magnificent. The tughra was the official signature used by the Ottoman sultans, and was one of Islam's most unique and sophisticated motifs.

swansong of the age of galleys, the distinctive 100 to 150 foot-long vessels rowed by slaves, convicts, or prisoners. The two sides engaged just off the western coast of Greece. Along with the galleys of the Ottomans, whose rowers were mostly Christian prisoners, came others from Egypt and Algeria. Yet it was the Christian side, consisting of a hodgepodge of Italian, German, and Spanish vessels, including galleys and frigates, that triumphed.

The victory provided a major boost to morale in Europe, Nevertheless, the Sultan was not too disturbed by the defeat, remarking philosophically: "They have cut off my beard, but it will grow again!" He was right, and in fact it would not be until more than a century later that the tide would begin to turn in Europe's favor.

Nevertheless, by the end of the seventeenth century, after a succession of sultans, the Ottoman Empire had begun to show clear signs of its ultimate decline. Increasingly outpaced by major developments in the West, the threat it posed to a rapidly modernizing Europe had begun to wane. By the middle of the following century the glorious "Sublime Porte" had now been renamed the "Sick Man of Europe."

Militarily too, the Ottomans were falling behind the West—in terms of strategy, tactics, and command they had become outclassed. Their huge armies were geared to large brass artillery for long sieges yet also held a preference for hand-to-hand combat, and so were increasingly less effective against the latest technological advances developed in Europe such as the flintlock musket and the mobile field gun.

This became evident in 1683, when Sultan Mehmet IV made another failed attempt to topple the Austro-Hungarian Empire by taking its capital. The second siege of Vienna was lifted when the Polish army under the control of John Sobieski attacked the Ottomans from behind and routed them. The siege had resurrected the Holy League (an alliance of national armies united by the Pope in Rome), now comprised of Venice, Austria, and Poland, with additional help from Safavid Persia. A series of setbacks followed which led to the first major loss of Ottoman territory. In 1699, with the Treaty of Karlowitz, the Ottomans were forced to relinquish control of Hungary to the Austro-Hungarians. A further treaty saw them obliged to cede territories in the Balkans.

Further disrupting the balance of power was the fast-emerging nation of Russia. From the second half of the eighteenth century, Russia took a keen interest in certain Ottoman possessions. The Black Sea, surrounded almost entirely by Ottoman territories, was a major route out to the Mediterranean. Given that rivers flowing into the Baltic Sea or the Arctic Ocean were liable to be icebound for a good part of the year, Russia needed the Black Sea as a warm-water outlet for trade, especially during the winter months. In order to ensure access, the Russian Tsar Peter the Great and his successors engaged in several wars against the Ottomans.

By the middle of the nineteenth century, although Russia had become the dominant force in the Black Sea, it could not escape the fact that its ships still needed to pass through the narrow straits of the Bosphorus and Dardanelles, which lay squarely under Ottoman control, in order to reach the Mediterranean. Attempting to strengthen its influence in the region, Russia played on shared

Shamyl—Defender of the Caucasus

Shamyl was the nineteenth-century leader of the peoples of the Northern Caucasus in their resistance against Imperial Russia and its expansion southwards. Born in Daghestan in 1797, he took a leading part in preaching jihad against the invading Russians. His unparalleled bravery in battle was matched by his spiritual learning and ability to form alliances among the fragmented Mountaineer peoples of the Great Caucasus Mountains. He soon found himself elected as the spiritual and military leader of the North Caucasians, which included the Avars and Chechens.

His armies of Sufi warriors, known as *murids*, held off the Russian Empire for a quarter of a century, from 1834 to 1859. His fight for independence made him a loose ally of Britain and France during the Crimean War (1853-55) and brought him considerable fame in Europe. However, Russia subsequently turned its full forces on the Caucasus and the North Caucasians gradually gave up their resistance. Shamyl himself was captured in 1859. The remainder of his life was spent in exile in St Petersburg and Kiev, and he died in Mecca while on Hajj in 1871.

Shamyl was the last and greatest of a long line of Islamic leaders who united the North Caucasians in more than eighty years of resistance against the Russians. Their bloodiest encounters with the Tsarist forces tended to take place in the less mountainous region of northern Chechnya, a pattern we still see today. The first commander was known only as Elisha Mansour. He is believed to be an Italian Jesuit priest sent to convert the Greeks in Anatolia to Catholicism during the latter half of the eighteenth century. To the anger of the Pope, he soon converted to Islam, and was sent by the Ottoman Sultan to organize Caucasian resistance against the Russians. His forces were finally defeated at the battle of Tatar-Toub in 1791.

Shamyl himself was a disciple of the Naqshbandi Sufi Ghazi Mollah, a fellow Avar from Daghestan. In the 1820s Ghazi Mollah organized a movement that grew into full-scale resistance against the Russians, frequently humiliating them in incidents such as that at Tsori, a mountain pass, where 4,000 Russian troops were held up for three days by a barricade manned by only two Chechen snipers. Ghazi Mollah died in a siege at Ghimri, at which Shamyl himself was one of only two *murids* who survived and escaped.

cultural and linguistic traits with many of the peoples living in Ottoman territories. As an Orthodox Christian country (distinct from the Catholics and Protestants of Europe), Russia consequently embraced the role as protector of Orthodox Christians living under the Turks. During the nineteenth century it also began to make much of its affinity with the Slavic-speaking peoples of the Balkans— including the Serbs, Croats, and Bulgarians—and involved itself in their struggles on a number of occasions.

The Ottomans also had to face considerable internal challenges to their rule. In Saudi Arabia, they faced mounting opposition from the followers of Wahhabi, an eighteenth-century thinker and founder of a very influential Islamic revival movement which openly challenged the Ottoman authorities. Wahhabi was responsible for converting the Saud tribe of central Arabia, which, during the nineteenth century, waged major military campaigns in the region that seriously undermined Ottoman control. (Wahhabism is still dominant in Saudi Arabia today.)

Colonization of Ottoman Egypt

The prized territory of Egypt proved especially problematic. Bogged down by their European and Persian wars, the Ottoman Sultans had given little attention to the day-to-day governing of the province. While they supplied governors and maintained a garrison of Janissaries, the Ottoman authorities simply had allowed the ruling Mamluk dynasty to continue keeping law and order. Mamluk leaders even went by the Turkish title of "Bey" meaning "Ruler," and effectively held sway over the land. Living up to their reputation, they proved troublesome, especially under Ali Bey, between 1760 and 1772. The unruly Mamluk finally ceased sending tribute to the Ottomans and began minting his own coins—a clear enough declaration of independence. By the end of the eighteenth century, Egypt was in a state of near anarchy, severely weakened by years of civil war and incompetent leadership. The chronic instability that plagued the province made it easy prey for the European powers, and it was here that the West took its first major step in the colonization of the Muslim world.

Driven by dreams of empire as well as as hampering British access to India and the East, France invaded Egypt in 1798. Leading the campaign was Napoleon Bonaparte, who attempted unsuccessfully to convince the Egyptian religious leaders and notables of France's benign intentions. In fact, he announced, France had come to put an end to years of misery caused by the Mamluks. Taking control of Cairo, the French began to set up their new administration. With a view to including Egyptians in the governing process, they invited the Ulema (the country's highly influential religious leaders) and other key figures to participate in central and regional councils.

The French had arrived with high hopes for their intended colony. Accompanying their large army was what could best be described as a cultural battalion, comprising no less than 167 eminent scholars, scientists, and artists whose assignment was to investigate and record the country's past and present. The fruit of their labor was to be one of the most extensive works ever published on the country, a twenty-four-volume publication entitled *La Description de l'Égypte* ("The Description of Egypt") published between 1809 and 1813. Its evocation of the art, architecture, and customs of this ancient seat of civilization created such a stir in Europe that soon there was a continent-wide craze for all things Egyptian. Items such as clothing, furniture, and pottery were decorated with hieroglyphs, pyramids, sphinxes, and other motifs.

Yet the whole venture was doomed to failure, faced as it was with popular rebellion and a joint British and Ottoman force sent expressly to oust the French. A foray into Ottoman-controlled Palestine had similarly failed after French troops were felled by malaria and dysentery. After a mere three years, Napoleon was forced to withdraw his troops and abandon Egypt.

The invasion of Egypt had severely dented Ottoman prestige, yet in their attempt to remedy the situation they had unwittingly paved the way for a ruthless Muslim Albanian leader by the name of Muhammad Ali to seize the reins of power there.

Muhammad Ali had originally led an Ottoman-paid contingent to help eject the French, but since he clearly was the only one who could bring a semblance of order to the region in the ensuing anarchy, the Sultan in Istanbul was forced to accept his appointment as Pasha, or "Leader," of Egypt. Despite his new domain technically being a vassal state of the Ottoman Empire, Muhammad Ali was a law unto himself. He went on to found a dynasty that would be receptive enough to open the country up to European influences, yet at the same time was far too easily manipulated by foreign governments, a fact that allowed British colonization to enter through the back door.

The ambitious Muhammad Ali was eventually brought to heel before he could overrun Istanbul itself—but not by the Ottomans alone. It took concerted threats by the European powers, who were sensitive to the effects on the balance of world power should the Sick Man of Europe fall.

After the construction of the Suez Canal, which connected the Mediterranean with the Red Sea, thereby creating a much quicker route to markets in East Africa, Persia, and especially India, Great Britain came to see Egypt's security as paramount to its overseas trade and acted accordingly. After one of Muhammad Ali's successors almost single-handedly bankrupted the country in the 1870s, both Britain (by now the Canal's owner), as well as France (which had overseen the Canal's construction), seized control of the country's finances. From now on Egypt's rulers would come under their control.

Egypt's downfall also served to highlight the lengths to which European powers would go to secure their economic interests and satisfy their hunger for cheap raw materials and profitable markets for their products. Having colonized Egypt in all but name, the British government began to maximize cotton production in Egypt, where the crop could be grown cheaply and exported to the British textile mills. At the same time, they levied considerable taxes that made Egyptian products unprofitable, ensuring that the domestic textile industry was uncompetitive. The influx of foreign capital into Egypt was phenomenal. By the early twentieth century it was estimated that some 70 percent of the country's stocks and shares was held by foreigners.

The Ottoman Decline

By the nineteenth century, the Ottomans found themselves struggling to contain ethnic rebellions, and their regional systems of government began to collapse like dominos. By the 1830s, the independent Kingdom of Greece had been formed, and as the nineteenth century progressed more Ottoman territories disappeared at an alarming rate.

The Russians, meanwhile, continued to chip away at Ottoman territories around the Black Sea, invading Bessarabia (the coastal area of the Ukraine from the River Danube to Moldova), as well as the North and South Caucasus, including Chechnya, Georgia, Armenia,

FRANCES MARTIN

Mosque of Muhammad Ali at the Citadel of Cairo, built in the nineteenth century.

and Azerbaijan. From this strategic crossroads between Europe and Asia, Russia, still seeking that elusive warm-water port, moved southwards into Persia, only to be blocked by the British, who controlled neighboring Afghanistan to the east.

The Western Europeans lost no time in grabbing territories for themselves. 1878 was a particularly crushing year for the Ottomans when the Europeans forced them to accept the terms of the Treaty of Berlin. Bosnia and Herzogovina were handed to Austria, while Romania, Serbia, and Montenegro gained their independence, and Bulgaria was given autonomy under Ottoman suzerainty.

In the following decades up to the beginning of the First World War, Italy took Libya, and France invaded the prized lands of Algeria, Tunisia, Lebanon, and parts of Syria on the pretext of defending Lebanese Christians and protecting sacred Catholic sites. Great Britain took the lion's share by casting further afield, seizing Malta, the Gulf Emirates, Aden, Oman, Cyprus, and Southern Arabia, in addition to keeping a tight control over Egypt and the Suez Canal zone, and by extension Sudan.

Economically, the Ottoman Empire also had run into into severe difficulties. This had been a gradual decline: from the fifteenth century onwards the Portuguese maritime explorers had opened up trade routes to India by sailing around Africa, eventually bypassing the Ottomans and depriving them of their European-Asian trade monopoly. Meanwhile, more and more manufactured goods flooded into the empire from a rapidly industrializing Europe, while the Ottomans struggled to produce just enough to maintain their own bloated tapestry of emerging nations.

Ottoman attempts to reverse the decline proved ineffective. Inspired by the American and French revolutions, Sultan Selim III (1789-1807), with the help of French advisers, set about modernizing the army on Western models, even adopting European-style uniforms. He immediately ran into difficulties, and in 1807 auxiliary troops, or *yamaks*, rebelled against the controversial uniforms. Threatened by a loss of power and privilege within the new system, the Janissaries joined them. In the next few years the Janissary crack troops executed many of the reformers among the Sultan's counselors and ministers, backed by a ruling of the Grand Mufti that such uniforms were contrary to Muslim law.

Selim was deposed and imprisoned. His relative Mustafa IV (1779-

1808) came to power briefly until his predecessor's supporters stormed the palace. There they discovered that Mustafa had ordered Selim to be strangled. The Janissaries dragged Mustafa from his throne and had him strangled with a bowstring, proclaiming as Sultan the Ottoman Prince Mahmud II (1784-1839).

It was the Janissaries' resistance to Westernizing reforms that proved their downfall. A new wave of reforms aimed at the army, backed up by a religious *fatwa*, or edict, that it was the duty of all Muslims to acquire military technology, provoked a fresh revolt by the Janissaries in 1826. They ran riot through Istanbul, pillaging and looting, backed by the Ulema who issued their own *fatwa* stating: "If unjust and violent men attack their brethren, fight against the aggressors and send them before their natural judge!" The Sultan's artillery commander made a last appeal to the rebels to surrender. On their refusal, he gave the order to open fire on them. Those who escaped were shot down as they fled. The barracks where many sought refuge were burned and those taken prisoner were brought before the Grand Vizier and hanged. The days of the Janissaries, the glory of Turkey's early days and the scourge of the country for the last two centuries, were finally over.

Between 1839 to 1876, the Empire underwent a period of modernizing reforms, known as the Tanzimat, which significantly weakened the Ulema's traditional hold over the institutions of justice and education. Yet, the attempt was ultimately destined to fail, and led instead to increased dependency on Europe. The result was a huge external debt that proved crippling.

Dawn of the Secular State

Sultan Abdulhamid II, the last Sultan effectively to rule over the Ottoman State, succeeded in temporarily reinvigorating the failing empire, but it was too late. The loss of territories ceded under the terms of the disastrous Treaty of San Stefano in 1878, which concluded the last of the Russo-Turkish wars and greatly increased Russia's influence in southeast Europe, combined with the overall steady attrition caused by European imperialism, left the integrity of the Empire in near tatters. Abdulhamid responded to the threat by reaffirming his position as Caliph, and began to actively promote Islamic unity.

Sensing the growth of Western-style nationalistic tendencies among his subjects, particularly among the Arab groups and Albanians, Abdulhamid hoped to head them off by creating a sense of Islamic solidarity geared at holding the empire together. But he soon had to cave in to external and internal pressures, particularly from a liberal reformist group, later dubbed the "Young Turks", and he reluctantly allowed a written constitution, which created a parliamentary system modeled on those in the West. For the first time in the history of the Empire, absolute Ottoman rule had been relinquished. But Abdulhamid abandoned democracy within a year, after new attacks on his borders by Russia and Britain.

Harshly criticized for repression, censorship, and paranoia of conspiracy, Abdulhamid was nevertheless effective in his Westernization of the Empire, concentrating on public works, economic development, education, and communications. The telegraph, which provided access to information from beyond the Empire's borders, also was useful to his network of spies, providing Abdulhamid with a means for controlling potential insurgencies from within.

This strengthening of nationalism had resounding consequences, not least for the sizable minority of Christian Armenians. Many of these were starting up revolutionary groups in response to a growing awareness of their own ethnic and regional national identities. Fearful of the threat of separatism and of Armenian alliances with European powers, Abdulhamid suppressed these insurgencies in the series of brutal massacres of 1894-1896, in which an estimated 300,000 Armenians were killed. This failed, however, to prevent separatist movements from springing up in the other corners of the empire.

The late 1880s saw the beginnings of the Young Turk movement. Made up primarily of military officers and rebels, they orchestrated a successful nonviolent coup d'état in 1908 designed to reinstate the constitution in the name of "Liberty, Justice, Equality, and Fraternity." Abdulhamid was deposed and his brother Mehmed V was released from prison as a token head of state.

The Young Turk era (1908-1922) introduced a modern political structure based on European models that deliberately merged a modernized Islamic tradition with European cultural influences, and went far beyond the technical achievements of the Tanzimat and of Abdulhamid II. The Young Turks anticipated and provided many of the initial programs of the modern Turkish Republic that followed by secularizing education and justice and taking the first steps toward social and economic democracy as well as the emancipation of women.

However, new nationalist terrorism and foreign attacks by Italy (Tripolitanian War, 1911) and the allied Balkan States (Balkan Wars, 1912-1913) led to the imposition of the autocratic rule of the Young Turk Triumverate: Enver, Talat, and Cemal. When the Young Turks first came to power, they turned their eyes eastward hoping to restore the glory of the greater Ottoman Empire. They abandoned the Pan-Islamism ideal of the Empire and instead embraced an international Pan-Turkism, the uniting of all Turkish-speaking peoples across the Middle East and Central Asia. With World War I ripping their already tattered Ottoman Empire apart and the appearance of numerous small states in the Balkans and Arabian Peninsula, the Young Turks decided to purify Turkey first, eliminating the non-Turkic nationalities from its soil. They soon realized that it could only be done forcefully.

Ethnic repression within the remaining borders found its logical, terrible conclusion in the Young Turks' massacre of the Christian Armenian minorities in 1915, which reprised the atrocities committed by Abdulhamid II twenty years before. The massacres between them saw up to a million Armenians and other minorities slaughtered and an innumerable number of survivors forcefully deported. Adolf Hitler took inspiration from both the Pan-Turkism ideology and the massacres, famously asking, in connection to his own genocidal policies, "Who still speaks nowadays of the extermination of the Armenians?"

Ataturk—The National Liberator

Fatefully, their decision to support Imperial Germany against the Allied forces of Britain and France had placed the Ottomans on the losing side of World War I. In the peace that followed the conflict, the defeated Empire was dismantled by the victorious Western Powers. In the 1920 Sevres Treaty, the Ottoman government was forced to sign a humiliating agreement to partition Turkey between the colonial powers.

As the Ottoman State entered its death throes, a young officer by the name of Mustafa Kemal, who would later be known as Ataturk

("Father of the Turks") emerged as the national liberator of the Turks. Actively involved in the Young Turk revolution of 1908, Ataturk went on to become a legendary hero of the Dardanelles and other fronts, and in 1919 he became the leader of the Turkish emancipation. Setting up a rival government in Ankara, with a small and ill-equipped army, he nevertheless launched series of successful campaigns against the Greeks who had made advances in Western Turkey, and the Armenians in the eastern provinces, all the time taking advantage of disagreements among the Allied forces.

By 1922, Ataturk had secured control over the Turkish mainland and, having overcome internal opposition, he immediately abolished the Ottoman dynasty. In July 1923, the Lausanne Treaty signed among others by Great Britain, France, Greece, Italy gave Turkish independence international recognition. A republic was proclaimed and Ataturk became its first president, declaring: "This nation has never lived without independence. We cannot and shall not live without it!"

The account of Ataturk's fifteen-year presidency of Turkey is a saga of dramatic modernization. With indefatigable determination, he created a new political and legal system within a distinctly secular state. His reforms took the religious elements out of government and education, gave equal rights to women, changed the alphabet and the attire to Western forms, and advanced the arts and the sciences, agriculture and industry.

Ataturk's rise to power not only saw the end of the Sultanate, but of the Caliphate too. The Ottoman Sultans had kept their title until the last Sultan Muhammad VI was deposed. He was succeeded briefly by a cousin, but in 1924 Ataturk officially abolished the Caliphate. A year later Husayn ibn Ali, King of Arabia, proclaimed himself Caliph, but he was forced to abdicate by Ibn Saud. Since then several pan-Islamic congresses have attempted to revive the Caliphate with little signs of acceptance by other Muslims.

The demise of the Ottoman Empire, therefore, along with the abolition of the Caliphate, sealed the fate of the last of the Islamic Empires. It proved not only to be a profoundly traumatic event for Muslims around the world, but also one that would permanently affect European and world affairs.

The Safavids
and Shi'ism—
Persia Reunified

Have you seen Esfahan, that city like Paradise,
That holy cypress, that soul-nourishing Eden;
That palace of the nation and that throne of government
That face of seven spheres, that eye of the seven lands?
—Jamal al-Din Isfahani

The Safavid dynasty, founded in 1501, held sway over Persia for nearly three centuries. Under the first Safavid Shah, Ismail (1486-1524), years of chronic instability brought about by warring regional tribes came to an end, and under subsequent Safavid Shahs, Persia went on to enjoy a major cultural and political revival. The secret of their success was Shi'ism, which, actively promoted by the Safavid state, became the key force shaping the distinctive identity of the Empire. Today, as a direct result of Safavid policies, Shi'ism remains a defining characteristic of present-day Iran, setting it aside from its Sunni neighbors. Throughout most of its history it was a major rival to the Sunni Ottomans, engaging in frequent wars that were a clear reminder of the profound divisions that ran through the Muslim world.

Shah Ismail came to power in 1501. He was the latest in a long line of leaders belonging to an illustrious Turkish-speaking family, most likely of Kurdish origin, which hailed from Ardabil in southern Azerbaijan. The Safavids controversially claimed to be descendants of the Twelfth Imam, and as leaders they were seen as playing an active and vital role in God's plan for the world.

One of Ismail's most famous ancestors was Safi al-Din of Ardabil (1252-1334), from whom the dynasty took its name. A holy ascetic Sufi, Safi al-Din was an immensely popular figure, both with the people and the rulers of his day, and he was credited with extraordinary powers that included the ability to make prophecies and work miracles. In 1301 he established a Sufi order that in time went from strength to strength, gaining in prestige to the extent that the family even could count on the support of the Mongols and possibly from Timur himself.

By the end of the fifteenth century,

Detail showing tile façade and dome of Masjid-i-Shaykh Lotfollah (built 1602-1619), in Esfahan, Iran. The mosque ranks among the finest examples of Safavid architecture.

Safi al-Din's descendants had become a highly militant and powerful force in western Persia and eastern Turkey. The order, previously Sunni, now openly embraced the Shi'i Islamic rite and became a channel for the popular following Ali enjoyed among both Shi'is and Sunnis, drawing strong Turkic tribal support from eastern Anatolia, the highlands of Armenia, and northern Syria. In its new-found militantism, its leaders launched the first jihad against Christians in the Caucasus.

Ismail's coming to power was seen as paving the way for the coming of the "Mahdi," or Messiah, in the prelude to the Day of Judgment. Yet the journey to the throne had been a hard-won undertaking. Ismail had spent several years imprisoned by the enemies of his father, Heydar. Believed by his followers to have been semi-divine, Heydar had been highly active in the campaigns against the Christians. His troops were known as the Qizilbash ("Red Heads") on account of the red turbans they wore, emblazoned with twelve folds that commemorated the Shi'i Twelve Imams

However, in 1488, after falling afoul of the leadership of the Aq-Qoyunlu, the dominant Turkic tribe that had established control in the region, Heydar was killed and members of his family were subsequently taken into custody. Managing to gain his freedom, the young Ismail was forced to lie low and wait for the chance to avenge his father's death. When he finally reached maturity, he proved to be the ablest of leaders and won a victory over the Aq-Qoyunlu at the Battle of Shurur in 1501. After securing Tabriz, he was proclaimed Shah of Persia. Further Safavid campaigns put a decisive end to the Aq-Qoyunlu and confirmed his new status as the ruler of the region.

From Tabriz, and later from their new capital at Esfahan, the Safavids oversaw a period of great empire building across Persia and surrounding regions. Ismail lost no time in imposing Shi'ism as the state religion and set into motion a massive and highly effective campaign to convert the predominantly Sunni population of his new empire. The move served to unite Persia behind a common banner that distinguished it from its Sunni neighbors, bringing it a sense of unity which had not been enjoyed since the days of the Sassanian Empire.

Pattern from a luster dish, from twelfth-century Persia.

Revival of Persian Fortunes

Under the Safavids, Persian art and literature were energetically promoted. Esfahan was transformed into a major cultural center whose influence radiated outwards across the empire and beyond. Esfahan became to the Shi'i world what Istanbul was to that of the Sunnis.

The Safavids reached their zenith under the rule of Shah Abbas I (1557-1629), who oversaw the construction of the finest Safavid architecture in Esfahan, which became his capital in 1598, transforming it into one of the world's largest and most spectacular cities. A huge city with a population of perhaps 600,000, it boasted 162 mosques, 48 *madrasas*, hundreds of caravanserais, and 273 public baths. The city also featured parks and magnificent avenues, some four kilometers long, lined by gardens and court residences, while trading was conducted in a spectacularly huge bazaar.

Persian economic fortunes revived dramatically after trade had almost ceased following the disintegration of its Il-Khanate Empire. Keen to boost the empire's commerce, especially the silk trade, Abbas I went out of his way to make conditions in Persia as attractive to European merchants as possible, encouraging governments to open embassies in Esfahan and even inviting Catholic orders to establish missionaries.

Safavid ruler, *c.* 1540.

A thriving industry developed in the production and export of fine Persian carpets and textiles such as silks and velvet. Potters excelled in ceramics, using their skills to great effect in the creation of the spectacular tile patterns that still can be seen adorning the surfaces of magnificent mosques and other buildings from the period.

Tile panel from a palace of Shah Abbas the Great.

The Safavid period also produced some of the most exquisite paintings, especially those used to illustrate the classics of Persian literature. Artists employed a dazzling use of color to bring their subjects to life, their pages bustling with detailed scenes featuring elegant human and animal figures and vibrant flora. Shah Ismail, himself an accomplished poet, did much to boost the artistic tradition by bringing back to Tabriz artists from the city of Herat (in modern Afghanistan) that he captured in 1510. Ismail's son, Shah Tahmasp, was himself an avid student of painting and spent a considerable amount of time studying art in Herat, which had become an artistic center under the ruling Timurid dynasty there. As a patron he developed an especially close relationship with his painters.

The Decline of the Safavids

Subsequent Safavid rulers failed to repeat Abbas I's successes and the Empire experienced a gradual decline. The wars against the Ottoman Empire and other enemies, combined with a chronic lack of leadership, took its toll on the Safavid state. The arrival of the eighteenth century saw Persia in a critical state, drifting under a succession of puppet shahs. In 1722, it was thrown into full-blown crisis following an invasion by Afghan forces under the leadership of Mir Mahmud of Kandahar. Only a few years previously his father, the governor of Afghanistan had proclaimed his independence. Mir Mahmud subsequently toppled the Safavid ruler, Tahmasp II, and had himself proclaimed Shah.

In the midst of the chaos, Tsar Peter the Great of Russia seized the moment to pursue his imperial ambitions and gain a slice of Safavid territory, all conveniently under the pretext of supporting the overthrown shah. Marching southwards along the western coast of the Caspian, his army took a number of key cities and towns in northwestern Persia, including Baku (today the capital of the Republic of Azerbaijan). However, in an about-face, to avoid a major confrontation with the Ottomans, Russia subsequently signed a treaty with the Ottoman sultan in 1724, in which the two powers granted themselves the right to a sizeable share in western Persian territories.

The Peacock, once a symbol of Imperial Persia—and so it was said that the Shah ruled from the "Peacock Throne."

Meanwhile, in Esfahan, Mir Mahmud had unleashed a vicious campaign of violence, massacring Safavid royal family members along with anyone else who incurred his wrath. Esfahan would never recover its glory. Afghan ambitions were only checked in 1729, when they found their match in

Nadir, a general belonging to the Afshar tribe of Khorasan. Nadir subsequently had Tahmasp II restored to the throne in Esfahan. By the mid 1730s, he had also recovered lands lost in northwestern Persia to the Ottomans and Russia.

In 1736, Nadir took the throne for himself and was crowned Shah. He went on to establish a sizeable empire, making gains from Kandahar to Delhi, where the Mughal Emperor was forced to pay tribute. Furthermore, as war resumed with the Ottomans, Nadir Shah scored another series of victories. A Sunni himself, he also nurtured dreams of imposing orthodoxy on the Persian empire, but to no avail. He was assassinated in 1747.

After Nadir Shah's death his empire descended into anarchy as various contenders fought for the throne. The once centralized Safavid empire now began to disintegrate. While a new dynasty, the Qajar, took power in Persia during the latter part of the century and survived until the 1920s, attempts to revive the Iranian empire were destined to fail.

The Khan's Palace in Baku, Azerbaijan.

The Mughals in India

"The impact of the invaders from the northwest and of Islam on India had been considerable. A foreign conquest, with all its evils, has one advantage: it widens the mental horizon of the people and compels them to realize that the world is a much bigger place than they had imagined."
—Pandit Jawaharlal Nehru, India's first Prime Minister 1947-64

India before the Mughals

When Islam finally blossomed on the Indian Subcontinent, it did so in a spectacular way, giving rise to the great empire of the Mughals, who in the sixteenth century united the whole of northern India under Muslim rule. Traditional Hindu beliefs would prove exceedingly hard to dislodge, and Muslims would always remain a minority. Yet the early Mughal rulers entered into a dynamic and inventive relationship with their new subjects, exerting a strong influence while often proving to be remarkably receptive and sensitive to their environment.

Islam had been slow to take root in India. Its spread in the Subcontinent proved not to be the result of the efforts by the Caliphate in Baghdad, but of several of the new independent Muslim kingdoms that had been forming in Central Asia. In fact, once they had reached into Persian Central Asia during the early Arab conquests, the Umayyad Caliphs showed little inclination to follow through and claim the Indian Subcontinent for Islam. Arab forces had reached Sind as early as 644, but had nothing positive to report back to the Caliphate. However, provoked by attacks on Arab trade ships passing Sind, the Umayyad governor of Iraq sent expeditions into the region, which was finally brought to heel in 712. Beyond this, there were no other major thrusts into India, and, for the time being at least, Islam would remain confined to the limits of Sind.

A key player who helped pave the way for Muslim rule in northern India was Mahmud of Ghazna (971-1030), the ruler of a kingdom centered on the city of Ghazna (in modern Afghanistan). Mahmud, whose rule had been sanctioned by the Abbasid Caliphate, was a staunch Muslim who launched a sustained series of violent campaigns into Indian territories. Riding over the dramatic mountain passes of Afghanistan, his cavalry thundered down into the plains looting Hindu cities and destroying temples.

The wealth he amassed enabled him to develop Ghazna into one of the great cities of the eleventh-century Islamic world, from where he ruled over an empire whose territories reached into Iran and took in the Punjab region of India. In the tradition of great Muslim leaders, he became a great patron of architecture and the arts, enticing the likes of luminaries such as the thinker Al-Biruni and the great Persian poet Firdawsi (*c.* 940–1020), who authored the *Shah Nameh* ("The Book of Kings"), considered one of the world's great epics, some 60,000 verses that recount the history of Persia from mythical times.

However, the Ghaznavid dynasty founded by Mahmud faced a steady decline, eventually ruling over a diminished kingdom from the city of Lahore (in modern Pakistan) where they were eventually overrun by a rival dynasty in 1186.

The next significant event in the development of Islam in India was the capture of Delhi by Muhammad of Ghor in 1192. It led to the creation of the so-called Sultanate of Delhi, a succession of unstable Muslim dynasties that ruled between 1210 and the arrival of the Mughals in 1526. Extending across the north of India, the Sultanate was vulnerable to attacks from the Mongols, while internally, the Sultans faced a tough job keeping the population, the overwhelming majority of whom were Hindu, under control.

Nevertheless, during the fourteenth century under the rule of the ferocious Muhammad Tughluq, who founded his own dynasty (1325-98), the power of Delhi was acknowledged even in the far south. In Muslim-held India, the language of the court was Persian. While some Hindus had begun to convert to Islam and were thereby able to take up official posts previously denied them, as part of an ongoing effort to strengthen the regime, educated foreign Muslims often found themselves in great demand as judges, administrators, academics, and other highly rewarded positions.

The great traveler Ibn Battuta described Delhi as:

> . . . the metropolis of India, a vast and magnificent city, uniting

beauty with strength. It is surrounded by a wall that has no equal in the world, and is the largest city in India, nay rather the largest city in the entire Muslim Orient.

Ibn Battuta was lucky to have an audience with the Sultan Tughluq whom he described as a man who was "the fondest of making gifts" but also "of shedding blood." He described the Sultan's palace at Delhi as:

> . . . containing many doors. At the first door there are a number of guardians, and besides it trumpeters and flute-players. When any emir or person of note arrives they sound their instruments and say "So-and-so has come, so-and-so has come!" The same also takes place at the second and third doors. Outside the first door are platforms on which the executioners sit, for the custom amongst them is that when the Sultan orders a man to be executed, the sentence is carried out at the door of the audience hall, and the body lies there over three nights.

The Tughluq dynasty proved short-lived, and soon more upheavals befell the region. In 1398, Timur's Mongols sacked Delhi, leaving the city in ruins. The shattered Sultanate limped on until finally succumbing to the forces of another powerful invader from the north, Babur, founder of the great Mughal dynasty.

The Age of the Mughals

Babur (1483-1530), was a descendant of Genghis Khan on his mother's side and Timur on his father's. A native of Ferghana in Central Asia, he spent his early career unsuccessfully attempting to conquer Samarkand (Timur's old capital). Giving up on this, he turned his sights instead on the Punjab and the northern regions of the Indian Subcontinent. Seizing the Afghan cities of Kabul, which he made his capital, and Kandahar, he began to launch raids on the Punjab.

Babur's opportunity to gain power in India was handed to him by the governor of Lahore, who called on his help to keep the ruler of the Sultanate of Delhi, Ibrahim, at bay. Babur was happy to oblige and, demonstrating his brilliant military leadership and tactical use of artillery in April 1526 at Panipat (in northwestern India), he soundly defeated the Sultanate's forces. Reminiscing about the battle, Babur declared that he had placed his "foot in the stirrup of resolution and hands on the reins of confidence in God!"

The victorious Babur subsequently declared himself Sultan of Delhi and Agra, which went on to become two of the greatest Mughal cities, and laid the foundation of the greatest Muslim dynasty ever seen in Asia.

The name Mughal, a variant of Mongol, gives away the Central Asian origins of the dynasty. True to their roots, Babur and his generals never entirely felt at home in India and missed their native Central Asia. Indeed, when they had first arrived in India, Babur had had a tough time persuading his army not to head back to the cool hills of home before the stifling Indian summer heat set in.

Babur was also a distinguished poet, and his writing was infused with a profound sense of nostalgia and a less than positive view of his adopted country. Holding the northern Indian people to be unfriendly, he criticized their poor architectural skills, lack of water channels, gardens, hot baths and houses with running water. He also lamented the absence of fine horses and dogs, iced or cold water, candles, and melons. Nevertheless, he was destined to live out his final days in India and died in Agra in 1530.

He left his son Humayun (1508-56) to carry the Mughal torch, but the new emperor got off to a decidedly shaky start when he lost the realm to Sher Khan, a powerful general who had served under Babur. Sher Khan subsequently established his own short-lived dynasty in Northern India. Humayun was forced to seek refuge in Safavid Persia, and with the help of the Shah, Tahmasp, and a Persian force, he eventually succeeded in wresting his empire back.

Yet he was destined never to achieve greatness. By all accounts partial to opium, he tripped down the steps of his private astronomical observatory after gazing the stars (he was a keen astronomer). Suffering a blow to the head, Humayun died in 1556. Nevertheless, he left India a great legacy in the form of his thirteen-year-old son by his Persian wife, Hamida Banu Begum. The young Jalal al-Din Muhammad Akbar, known to history simply as Akbar (meaning "the Greatest" in Arabic), went on to enjoy a lengthy rule that saw the creation of an empire stretching from Pakistan across northern India to Bengal in the west. It was said that Akbar was capable of riding 240 miles in twenty-four hours to surprise and defeat a rebellion.

From the outset, Akbar, who married a Hindu princess from Jaipur, was reconciliatory towards his non-Muslim population and vociferously opposed to religious intolerance. He set about appointing local upper-caste Rajput governors and officials, and gave the post of revenue minister to a Hindu who oversaw a system of taxation that was generally fair, having avoided the excesses shown by so many other rulers. Hindus took up most of the lower posts in the Mughal administration. While the better part of the higher posts were taken up by Muslims, a good many were filled by non-Muslims too.

The Mughal Emperor Humayun.

In the north, defeated Rajput chiefs were also made governors or conferred honors and granted privileges that were enjoyed by Muslim noblemen.

Against a great deal of opposition from Muslim nobles Akbar ordered the abolition of the unpopular extra taxes incurred by non-Muslims, notably the *jizya* poll tax. He also prohibited Muslims from slaughtering cows so as not to offend Hindu sensibilities, opposed slavery, did away with the death penalty for apostasy, replaced the Islamic lunar calendar with the solar calendar, and even allowed women to keep their own faith when marrying Muslims.

Akbar's profound interest in religion led him on a personal and highly controversial quest to fuse together the diverse religions of the empire, gathering together Muslim, Hindu, Jain, Christian (including Jesuit priests from Goa), and Zoroastrian scholars to debate the subject. Interestingly, Akbar was illiterate, and could not resist placing that fact in a religious context by pointing out that so too were the prophets, including Muhammad. As such, he maintained, it was a great attribute and he went so far as to recommend that families benefit by keeping one son illiterate.

Ever adventurous and highly unorthodox in his religious views, Akbar even went so far as to create his own eclectic faith, "Din-i-Ilahi" ("Divine Faith"), which was suffused with the teachings of

Mughal Architecture

Humayun's Tomb, Delhi. Built between 1565 and 1569, using red sandstone and white marble, it is considered to be the prototype of the Taj Mahal.

Below: A view of the Jantar Mantar, Delhi—a complex of structures built to observe the movements of the sun, moon and planets. Built by Sawai Jia Singh II of Jaipur (1699-1743), an astronomer and a nobleman in the Mughal court, its aim was to correct the astronomical errors of less reliable instruments of the time. Yet its promise was never fulfilled. By the time it was completed the Mughal Empire was already in decline.

ALL PHOTOS LAURIE MARTIN/FRED JAMES HILL

An elegy in marble—the fabulous Taj Mahal Mausoleum, built on the orders of Emperor Shah Jahan to house the grave of his beloved Queen Mumtaz Mahal.

certain Sufi saints who had greatly impressed him. It was quite some way removed from orthodoxy and the rigors of the Sharia. Not surprisingly, his experiment did little to endear him to the Ulema, who found his heretical ideas thoroughly unpalatable.

Sufi mystics had already found a fertile ground in the religious climate of India. Their teachings had found a great deal of resonance in the region and played an important role in bridging the gap between Islam's strict monotheism and Hindu polytheistic beliefs. Many spiritual and dogmatic parallels were drawn between the two religions, allowing a process of syncretism to develop that is still very much alive to this day.

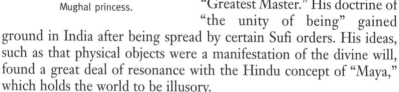

Mughal princess.

A major influence on Islam in India was the Spanish-born Ibn al-Arabi (1165-1240), a highly controversial Sufi thinker and author, known to his supporters as Al-Shaykh al-Akbar, the "Greatest Master." His doctrine of "the unity of being" gained ground in India after being spread by certain Sufi orders. His ideas, such as that physical objects were a manifestation of the divine will, found a great deal of resonance with the Hindu concept of "Maya," which holds the world to be illusory.

The Muslim-Hindu relationship was not simply one-sided. In time, Hindu traditions also began to be incorporated into Sufi rituals and practices in India, including local music and the discipline of yoga. Sufis also adopted the regional language, Hindi, which evolved into one of the great Muslim languages, Urdu.

The Mughals also left India a legacy of spectacular architecture, the greatest examples of which were constructed during the reigns of Akbar (1556-1605) and Shah Jahan (1628-58). Akbar's reign also saw the construction of Humayun's Tomb, built between 1565 and 1569 by his widow—she herself was later buried there with her husband. The superb monument still stands in Delhi. The magnificent construction is built of red sandstone inlaid with white marble. While

Hindu "kiosk" (on the towers) belong to the Hindu tradition, the building features Persian arches and is primarily Islamic.

Humayun's Tomb is generally considered to be the prototype of another great Mughal monument, one which has deservedly earned the reputation as being among the finest architectural gems in the world—the Taj Mahal. Commissioned by Shah Jahan, under whose rule Mughal architecture experienced its Golden Age, the spectacular Taj Mahal was constructed in Agra between 1632 and 1653. It was built in memory of the Emperor's beloved wife, Mumtaz Mahal, who died while giving birth to their fourteenth child in 1631. The project brought together expert craftsmen from around India, including Delhi and Lahore, as well as from Baghdad, Shiraz, and Bukhara. On his death, Shah Jahan was laid to rest there as well.

The Decline of the Mughals

Akbar's policies were continued by his successors Jahangir and Shah Jahan, but under the rule of the latter's son, Aurangzeb (1618–1707), there was a dramatic change of attitude. For Aurangzeb and his supporters, things had become far too lax for their liking. His response was the introduction of sweeping reforms that would see a major reversal of his predecessors' policies, zealously promoting Islam by reintroducing the poll tax on Hindus, reinstating the Muslim calendar, and enforcing Sharia law.

While Aurangzeb's rule saw the Mughals at the peak of their power, his death marked the beginning of the steady decline of the empire. Heavy-handed treatment by the authorities sparked off revolts by Hindus and Sikhs (Aurangzeb had had the ninth Sikh guru executed for refusing to embrace Islam and ordered temples destroyed), leading to ever greater tensions between the rulers and their subjects.

Amid such challenges, Great Britain, through its East India Company, was able to increase its influence in the region and by the end of the eighteenth century had effectively gained control over the whole of India. The Mughal emperors now became little more than puppets. In 1857, the British government finally stepped in and assumed direct control of the country, assigning the once-great dynasty to history.

Muezzin in winter calling the faithful to prayer from a
minaret in Kazan, the capital of Tatarstan, in Russia.

Islam in the Twentieth and Twenty-first Centuries

The first President of the republic of Turkey, Kemal Ataturk, demonstrates the new Turkish alphabet.

Creation of the Nation-States

"Turkestan, Afghanistan, Transcaspia, Persia—to many these words breathe only a sense of utter remoteness, or a memory of strange vicissitudes and of moribund romance. To me, I confess, they are pieces on a chessboard upon which is being played out a game for the domination of the world."
—Lord Curzon, Viceroy of India and British Foreign Secretary (1898)

As the twentieth century dawned, the great Muslim empires had declined or simply disappeared and practically the whole of the Islamic world lay under colonial rule. The nineteenth century had seen Muslim lands fall one after another under the sway of the European powers. The Ottoman Empire had shrunk drastically, the empire of the Mughals had been replaced by British colonial rule, Persia had lost its Caucasian territories, and elsewhere such as in Central Asia, Africa, and Indonesia, European colonial administrators had set up governments.

While the direct and indirect effects of colonialism on the Islamic world varied considerably, overall it left a legacy of bitterness, the scars of which are very much in existence today. The very word "imperialism" remains highly charged and figures greatly in Muslim protests against the West. Many of the Islamic world's current problems are perceived to be the direct result of past and present interference by non-Muslim Western powers in Muslim affairs.

From Colonialism to Independence

The West was by no means interested in mere territorial acquisition, but had pressing economic agendas. Since the explosion of the Industrial Revolution, Europe had developed a hunger for cheap raw materials and profitable markets for their products, and European governments ensured that terms of trade worked in their favor. Flooded by cheap imports, the local businesses in the colonies, which were usually hobbled by punitive taxes, simply went bankrupt. Colonial powers also established a tight grip over key sectors such as banking, communications (railways, ports, roads), and valuable natural resources, such as oil, and it was European investors who reaped the greatest rewards.

During the colonial period the physical presence of foreign powers in their lands was the source of much resentment to Muslims, but it was not the only concern. What proved more divisive in the long run was the creation of a new Europeanized, mostly indigenous, social elite that was cultivated and protected by the West.

Educated in Western schools and in European languages, this hybrid class was charged with manning the Western institutions of law and government that were implanted into the colonized countries. Of course, Western law and government had not simply been imposed where previously there had been chaos—Muslim populations already had their own well-established systems of law.

Most European innovations never filtered down through the population. For the overwhelming majority, life was harsh under colonial rule, and more often than not spent languishing in abject poverty. Nor did Western customs have much impact. While the ruling and Westernized intellectual elite might meet in European-style restaurants, sporting Western suits and speaking French or English, the majority of the population lived much as they had done for centuries and continued to wear traditional forms of dress, speaking only their native languages.

As the colonial powers left, they did what they could to ensure that the ruling elite they had cultivated would remain favorably disposed and safeguard their interests. Yet they also left the political make-up of the world radically altered. In the post-colonial era, the Islamic world was transformed beyond all recognition. Most of the Muslim states that exist today simply did not exist prior to the twentieth century.

The dismantlement of the remainder of the Ottoman Empire saw the Turkish state restricted to its present form of Turkey, but elsewhere spawned a myriad of new Arab states. Persia is now reduced to its present form as the Republic of Iran, shorn of lands traditionally under its sway, such as the Southern Caucasus which ultimately gave rise to the Republic of Azerbaijan, a culturally Muslim country, and the Republics of Georgia and Armenia, both with mainly Christian populations.

The Partition of India

When the British granted independence to colonial, multireligious India, attempts to forge an inclusive society of Muslims and non-Muslims failed at every level. Liberty came at a terrible price, accompanied as it was by a humanitarian catastrophe. In 1947, the Subcontinent was partitioned, creating two states: one Hindu—India, and the other Muslim, split into two—West Pakistan and East Pakistan (1,000 miles apart, separated by India). But millions of Hindus were left on Muslim territory and vice-versa, and the event led to one of the greatest mass migrations of people in history as they crossed the borders, followed by widespread bloodshed as Hindus and Muslims turned on each other with a vengeance. (Today India remains home to 120 million Muslims, while 2.18 million Hindus remain in Pakistan.) Muslim nationalism then proved too weak to hold the two culturally and linguistically diverse Pakistans together, and in 1971 the eastern half broke away to form Bangladesh, resulting in a bloody civil war.

The national flag of Pakistan is typical for a modern Islamic state: its colors are dark green and white. The white band to the left represents the minorities of the country while the main green field represents the Muslim majority. The crescent represents progress as well as the crescent of Islam, while the five-rayed star symbolizes light and knowledge.

To this day, partition of the Subcontinent has left a legacy of particular bitterness between Pakistan and India. Having both achieved the status of nuclear powers in the 1990s, military confrontation between the two countries took on an alarming new dimension. A particular flashpoint is their seemingly intractable conflict for control over the northern province of Kashmir.

India was partitioned shortly after independence to create the modern states of India, with its Hindu majority, and the Islamic state of Pakistan—which itself fragmented to give yet another Islamic country, Bangladesh. Elsewhere in Africa and the Far East Islamic states mushroomed as the European powers abandoned their colonies.

The new borders in which Muslims found themselves confined for the purposes of building nation-states were mostly not of their making but reflected the interests of the West. In addition to this, many Muslim populations found themselves under new governments based on the Western model that had either been salvaged from the colonial days or introduced hastily and with little debate.

Islam in Africa South of the Sahara

The countries of North Africa, such as Morocco and Egypt, have been part of the Islamic world virtually since the birth of the religion—but to the south, beyond the huge wastes of the Sahara desert that divide the continent, the presence of Islam is more complex.

Very broadly speaking, Islam spread south into sub-Saharan Africa through a network of Muslim traders and the communities they established to feed goods back to the Mediterranean, Middle East, and the Indian Ocean. Their increasing prosperity soon led to intermarriages with the local communities. A growing wave followed of conversions by rival traders, anxious to tap into the lucrative business links of the newcomers. Two quite distinct processes then developed in the spread of the religion.

In **West Africa** the tendency was for the rulers of the many city-states, kingdoms and empires—such as Kano, Gonja, Mali, Songhai and Bornu—to convert to Islam. Sometimes these rulers came to power as a result of the support offered them by Muslim clerics, or Ulema. Yet, in the murky world of politics, rulers frequently found themselves pitted against the same Ulema who had helped them into power. A common cause of conflict was

The Mosque in Djenné, Mali, once a trading rival of Timbuktu, is the largest mud structure in the world. The Mosque was built in 1907—a distinctive turreted building with three minarets more than ten meters high and with structural wooden beams that protrude as decoration from its sides.

the Ulema's pushing for greater implementation of Islamic institutions. Jihad movements led by Ulema were commonplace, the most famous perhaps being that of Usumanu (Uthman) dan Fodio, whose jihad between 1804 and 1808 united the Hausa and Fulani peoples to create a new Islamic state, the Hausa-Fulani empire, in what is now northern Nigeria.

When the European colonial powers began their major expansion throughout the continent in the nineteenth century they tended to set Islam aside from other religions. A common policy was to co-opt Islamic rulers through indirect rule and to appoint members of the Ulema as regional officials. Northern Nigeria was one such region, where the British preserved and supported the Hausa Bakwai—or seven Hausa emirates—which still exist today as federal states within Nigeria.

Some of the modern nations created by the colonial powers south of the Sahara are considered politically and culturally to be Islamic states—Mauritania and Mali are good examples. Most of the other nations, however, such as Senegal, Côte d'Ivoire, Ghana, and Nigeria, are left with Muslim populations that, though significant, do not have any clear majority. Their systems of government are designed to balance the demands of Islamic, Christian, and traditional (animist) religions, but the reality has proved a constant, potential source of internal instability.

East Africa and **the Horn of Africa** are geographically closer to the Arabian heartland where Islam began, and so cultural as well as trade influences rapidly spread down the coast of the Indian Ocean. East African Muslims developed an urban culture that remained in the coastal regions and looked to Arabia, Iran, India, and the Far East for its commercial connections.

In many ways the spread of Islam in East Africa could be described as a social rather than political process, although a militant tradition had developed in the Horn of Africa as a result of the power struggles that started in the sixteenth century with the neighbouring Christian state of Ethiopia. It was only in the nineteenth century that Islam moved westwards into the interior, ironically following the new trade routes and territories established by the Christian Europeans. Constructive co-existence is practiced not only with other religions but also other forms of Islam, such as Shi'ism brought over by traders and merchants from North India.

Off the coast, in the Indian Ocean, the Muslim island of Zanzibar today forms an autonomous part of the mainly Christian Republic of Tanzania, but the division is firstly a political and economic one, a position highlighted by the 1964 Revolution that overthrew the ruling Sultan and, for a few years, turned Zanzibar into an independent Marxist (yet still Islamic) state.

Islam in **South Africa** is a small but vocal force that found its origins in the migration of freeman and slaves from Malaysia and the islands of the Indian Ocean from the eighteenth century onwards. As in East Africa, the modern Muslim population was also swelled by the arrival of merchants from the Indian Subcontinent.

The Muslims of the Soviet Union and Afterwards

While the first two decades following World War II saw most Islamic countries gain independence, there was a very substantial Muslim population that would languish for many years longer under the rule of the Soviet and Chinese Communist regimes. (It was estimated that there were well over fifty million Muslims living in the Soviet Union and some seventeen million in China by the 1980s.) For them the twentieth century would be an extremely difficult period, one in which they would have to face oppressive regimes that were ideologically opposed to Islam.

In Russia, Muslims were principally centered in the Caucasus, which was annexed in the first half of the nineteenth century, and Central Asia, where the khanates of Khiva, Bukhara, and Turkestan were forced to accept Russian domination from the 1860s onwards.

Under the Tsars, Muslims found themselves disadvantaged by Russian policies aimed at reinforcing Orthodox Christianity throughout the empire—forcing the process of Russification on its unwilling Muslim subjects. Ecclesiastical Boards were established to control Islam, by means of which the Russian government set its sights on eroding the authority of the Ulema, the Muslim religious leaders and scholars who were the bastion of Islamic values and who were perceived to be the most obvious threat to Russian rule.

Sharia law was undermined as the mullahs and *qadis* were limited to involvement in matters concerning family law such as marriage, divorce, and inheritance. Civil and criminal law was a matter for the Russian courts. Muslim clerics, who were required to pledge loyalty to the Tsar, were rewarded by receiving privileges of rank, such as exemption from taxes and from corporal punishment. Many such privileges also were extended to their children. Islamic literature was subject to Tsarist censorship and Muslim religious land was subject to confiscation.

The Russian Revolution of 1917 put an end to Imperial Russia and paved the way to the creation of the Soviet Union, whose authorities pursued an official policy of atheism. During the first years under the Soviet authorities, state policy towards Islam was somewhat measured and seen very much as part of a secularizing and modernizing process. The main targets of the new regime, therefore, were the Muslim civil

The Chechens

The end of the twentieth century saw a worsening of already poor relations between the Russian government and the Chechen people—Sunni Muslims who live in the nominally Russian territory of the North Caucasus, and whose character is typically Caucasian and quite unrelated culturally or linguistically to their Russian overlords. During the course of an ongoing struggle to liberate themselves from Russian domination, a number of attacks were carried out by splinter Chechen terrorist groups. Before long, the whole of the Chechen movement had become linked to the wider, international pattern of "Islamic terrorism"—a situation that has detracted from the very real issues concerning a people who have spent centuries living under oppression.

In fact the Chechens have been fighting a war of survival against Russia since 1722, when Tsarist forces attempted to conquer the Caucasus. Led by a series of Imams including the brilliant Sufi military commander Shamyl, the Chechens, vastly outnumbered, resisted the Russian forces for 142 years, before finally falling in 1864. They revolted again in 1877, after which Russia slaughtered almost half of the population.

After forcing the Chechens into the Soviet Union in 1921, Stalin made an agreement with them that in return for accepting Soviet authority they would be allowed to practice Sharia law and have full autonomy in domestic affairs. But Stalin soon began a program of genocide of the Chechens and related Ingush peoples. In 1944, he accused the Chechens of having helped the Nazis, even though the Germans never reached the region. As punishment, Stalin deported the Chechens to Central Asia and Siberia. The Soviet Census of 1939 counted 407,690 Chechens of whom 400,000 were forcefully moved, many in cattle trucks in the dead of winter. Huge numbers died in transit or in the gulag camps to which they were sent. They remained in the gulags until 1957, when Stalin's successor, Kruschev, finally allowed them to return home. In 1991, the Chechens declared themselves a sovereign nation. By December of 1994, Russian forces attacked Chechnya, beginning a humiliating and tragic chapter in Russian military history. The war ended in 1996 with a stalemate. More than 100,000 Chechens and 6,000 Russian soldiers were killed, most of the country was razed, and seventeen million land mines were scattered by Russian forces.

In September 1999, Russia re-invaded Chechnya. A few thousand Chechens held off 100,000 Russians until February, 2000, when the Chechens were forced to evacuate their capital, Grozny. They have been fighting a guerrilla war ever since. It is the most recent fulfillment of the fateful promise made by the leader of the Chechens to the Tsar in 1818 that the Russians would never experience peace so long as a single Chechen remained alive. As the writer Alexsandr Solzhenitsyn said, describing the conditions in the gulags: "There was one nation that would not give in, would not acquire the mental habits of submission—and not just individual rebels among them, but the whole nation to a man. These were the Chechens."

courts and the Islamic charitable foundations or *waqfs*—a key part of traditional society—which were nationalized.

However, after Lenin's death, Stalin took over the leadership of the Soviet Union, and he soon ordered an all-out assault on Islam. This time he targeted the religion's core institutions: the mosques and religious schools (*madrasas*). Predictably too, the Soviets attacked traditions such as the wearing of veils, a most visible cultural practice closely associated with Muslims of Central Asia, and polygamy—all of which were banned. As in all other aspects of Soviet life, a climate of

The Shir-Dar Madrasa in Samarkand (built 1619-1636; now in present-day Uzbekistan).

fear set in: any state official seen to be too lenient towards religion was vulnerable to charges of being a Pan-Islamicist and thus an enemy of the state, with many thousands becoming victims of Stalin's murderous purges during the 1930s.

The damage to religious life was immense. In Azerbaijan in the Caucasus, for example, there were an estimated 2,000 mosques and 786 Qur'anic schools at the beginning of Soviet rule, yet by the 1980s

Islam in Southeast Asia

Forming a significant part of Southeast Asia are the predominantly Islamic, secular nations of Malaysia, Singapore, Indonesia, and Brunei. They are part of a huge archipelago of thousands of islands that also includes the Phillipines, where there is a large Muslim population in the south. The state presence of Islam and Sharia law can take a range of forms depending on the sometimes volatile regional politics and economics.

The Malay peoples form the vast majority of the population of this tropical island world. Today they are also the largest ethnic group in the Islamic world, representing almost twenty percent of the world's Muslim population: about two hundred million Malay Muslims are found in Indonesia which is also the largest Muslim nation in the world. It is interesting to note that the Malays also comprise the largest Christian church in Asia—the Roman Catholic church in the Republic of the Phillipines, where ninety percent of the population of more than seventy million are Christian. Also the largest Protestant church in Asia is found among the Malay Bataks of northern Sumatra in Indonesia.

Before the coming of Islam, external influences were mainly from China and India, and Hinduism was the dominant religion for many. By the ninth century Islam had already reached the islands but it was slow to take hold. Sumatra was Muslim from the twelfth century, Java by the fifteenth, Borneo by the sixteenth. From these bases the religion spread throughout the rest of the archipelago.

Introduced by Arab, Indian, and Chinese merchants and mystic Sufis, conversion was through peaceful means and not conquest. From the fourteenth to the nineteenth centuries, there was no organized Muslim mission effort in the archipelago. It was almost a spontaneous movement. The type of Islam brought

by the merchants was spread through intermarriage with the local population. This removed the obstacle of approaching the people from a dominant cultural and religious background, which proved a problem for the Christian missions that accompanied the European colonial powers, such as the Dutch, who arrived on the scene in force from the sixteenth century onwards.

Part of the Islamic world, yet far from its great empires, the archipelago adapted its own indigenous religious beliefs to the new faith. As one early convert wrote: "So long as we let our children become Muslims they will

The Grand Mosque of the Sultan's Palace at Jogjakarta, Indonesia.

take care of the veneration of our souls. Ancestor worship is for this life; Islam is for the life to come." One of the main attractions to Islam was the opportunity to be liberated from the Hindu caste system. This was especially true for the lower classes and in places like Java it was typically the royal court that remained the last stronghold of Hinduism.

Islam could have been prevented from spreading further into areas that came under European hegemony, as happened with the arrival of the Catholic Spanish in the Phillipines. However, in other parts of Southeast Asia, the arrival of the Western powers had the opposite effect and instead boosted the spread of Islam, which now became a unifying forrce against the new rulers.

Common ethnic and cultural ties throughout the region have meant that there is a strong solidarity among the Muslims of the various states. In some areas, however, Islam has not been not accepted, generally for ethnic or territorial reasons. This has especially been the case with the non-Malay peoples, and, with the creation of the modern, post-colonial states, religious difference has fueled regional conflicts such as those of East Timor and Aceh with the Indonesian government. Conversely, it is the Muslims in the south of the Phillipines who have consistently fought against their own central government. In such cases it is difficult to assess the precise role played by religion, although it is clearly an important component of regional identity.

only fourteen Shi'i and two Sunni officially registered mosques remained. The number of registered clerics amounted to no more than seventy and there were no formal Islamic institutions left in the Caucasus. With such a shortage of clerics and mosques in Azerbaijan, Shi'is—who constituted an overwhelming majority there—and Sunnis even worshipped shoulder to shoulder as the same mullah performed the two different rites, which ironically helped to forge mutual tolerance and cooperation between the two creeds.

In the hostile climate, Islam was driven underground. While outward manifestations of Islam were banned, the belief in Islam continued to be expressed in private away from the reaches of the state. In the postwar decades, despite a relaxation of the widespread persecution of 1930s, there was no real change in the status of religion. Discouraging Islam continued to be an official concern right up until the final years of the Soviet Union. At academic institutions the teaching of atheism was set up with scientific and ideological fervor accompanied by a steady stream of anti-Islamic literature.

After the collapse of the Soviet Union in 1991, no less than six new independent republics with Muslim majorities were born—those of Azerbaijan, a majority Shi'i country, and the Sunni-dominated states of Uzbekistan, Kazakhstan, Kyrgyzstan, Tajikistan, and Turkmenistan—all of which proudly reclaimed their Islamic heritage.

Despite Western fears that they might become radical centers of fundamentalism and international terrorism, this has not happened. In fact these nations have maintained cordial political and economic relations with the West. Any problems of radicalism lie more in dealing with abuses by traditional power bases that continue to be propped up by the former Communist Old Guard and the Western oil and gas industries.

The Muslims of China

For the Muslim peoples living further East in the People's Republic of China, as for the country's other religious denominations, religious freedom has been precarious. China has two main Muslim ethnic groups, the Uighurs and the Huis.

The Uighurs speak a Turkic language and are concentrated in the northwestern Xinjiang (formerly called "Sinkiang" in the West) region of the country. Numbering close to ten million, their history is closely connected to the Central Asian peoples. When Xinjiang came under the direct rule of the Chinese Communists in 1949, it was estimated that around three-quarters of the population was Uighur, yet the official policy of settling ethnic Han Chinese in the region has had a disruptive effect on the local population—as have the authorities' rigorous programs of imposing Chinese language and culture, including Sinicization of Islamic names. The Chinese state is unwilling to relax its control because not only is the land of the Uighur Turks a key strategic area, bordering as it does the Former Soviet Union, but it is also a key oil-producing area.

In the 1990s, dissatisfaction with conditions under the Chinese regime led to riots in which Muslims demanded independence, which in turn led to a major crackdown by the authorities and curbs on religious freedom. It is perhaps significant that many Uighurs were among those who died or were arrested as a result of the infamous Tiananmen Square massacre of protesters by government troops in 1989.

The 1990s saw growing restrictions on religious freedom. Between 1991 and 2003, around 1,500 Xinjiang mosques were closed owing to claims by the authorities they were built without permission. Freedom of religion was allowed so long as worshippers stayed out of the political arena. Thirty Muslim nationalists accused of "openly agitating against government officials" were executed in 1997. This was a part of what the Chinese government refered to as their "anti-crime campaign" against separatists. At the same time, a crackdown on "illegal" religious activities surfaced. Chinese officials closed local mosques and Qur'anic schools, occurrences that sparked a period of unrest in the region.

The Huis perhaps have a less traumatic existence in the China of today. Thirteen hundred years ago, Arabs and Persians took commerce along the "Silk Road" into China. These first groups were the foundation of Chinese Muslims who became known as the Hui. As the most widely scattered of China's national minorities, the more than eight million Huis can be defined as both urban and rural, rich and poor. They have largely been assimilated into the cultures of the other Chinese people among whom they live, reflecting Chinese clothing, family life, education, work, sports, entertainment, folk art and even their social problems. However, many Hui people continue to hold steadfastly to their Arab-Persian ancestry, avoiding many Chinese lifestyle customs.

In urban centers, the Huis tend to cluster in their own communities within the city, similar to the ethnic groupings in cities such as New York. In rural areas, the Hui make their living as farmers and traveling merchants. Their outward Islamic practices are more evident in the urban Hui communities than in the rural areas.

There are some 40,000 mosques officially reported in China, and the government has offered the Hui somewhat preferential treatment, seeing them as important in cultivating relations with the Muslim world. Nevertheless, the Huis have not traveled an easy road in clinging to their religious heritage—in particular, they endured centuries of severe discrimination and violence between themselves and the Han Chinese from before the 1300s through the early 1900s.

A Revival of the Caliphate?

The decline—and in many ways, fragmentation—of the Islamic world and the dominance of the West have produced a variety of responses reflecting a whole array of regional and historical factors.

It is significant, however, that the Islamic world lacks any central authority, either in the form of a Caliphate or any other institution, that might bind Muslims together and help them reach a consensus on the way forward. During the nineteenth century, the Ottomans had strengthened their claims to the role of Caliph, a move that was met with a great deal of controversy. Sultan Abdulhamid II included in his constitution of December 1876 two articles declaring firstly that, "The Sublime Ottoman Sultanate, which possesses the Supreme Islamic Caliphate, will appertain to the eldest of the descendants of the house," and secondly that, "The Sultan, as Caliph, is the protector of the Muslim religion."

In order to boost his standing as Caliph, the Sultan sent envoys across the Islamic world. The responses, while respectful, were not always encouraging. Every region, every school of law, every sect had its valid reasons for promoting another line of Caliphs—or even denying their revival in the first place. Yet the vacuum created by the formal abolition of the Ottoman Caliphate by Ataturk, when he established the modern republic of Turkey in 1924, created a very real sense of loss in many parts of the Islamic world—especially in

Southeast Asia, including Indonesia and Malaysia—leading many to ask how it could be replaced.

In India two brothers, Muhammad Ali (1878-1931) and Shawkat Ali (1873-1938), headed a popular and highly influential Caliphate movement. The debate continued to gain ground, eventually leading to the first general Islamic Congress of 1924, which was held in Cairo to discuss the revival of a new Caliphate in accordance with the Sharia. It was attended by representatives from the Middle East, India, Indonesia, Malaysia, and elsewhere. It is notable that since most of these countries were under European colonial rule, the delegates came unofficially, and not as representatives of their governments. Pointedly, Muslims from Turkey, Iran, Afghanistan, and Russia did not attend the conference.

It proved a fruitless task, with the delegates failing to reach any decision on what would constitute an acceptable Caliphate. During the proceedings, political issues came to the fore and muddied the waters. King Fuad of Egypt (r. 1920-36) for instance, had his own ambitions to become the new Caliph: a prospect that pleased few. For his part, King Ibn Saud of Saudi Arabia (1880-1953) simply refused to send a delegate. He was busy establishing his personal control over the holy cities of Mecca and Medina, and was hardly enthusiastic over the prospect of losing his newly acquired influence through the creation of a superior spiritual office.

At the second conference held by the Congress of the Islamic World in Mecca in 1926, the driving issue was not the Caliphate but "the fate of Mecca" and the management of the Hajj pilgrimage to the Holy Cities. This arose due to Ibn Saud capturing Mecca and Medina from the Hashemite Sharif Husayn and effectively monopolizing control over access to the cities. The situation had caused much unease throughout the Islamic world, and Muslims from India led those who argued for international Islamic control over the region. Undeterred, the Saudi king convinced his critics, and his bid to control the Holy Cities was successful. Today this Saudi franchise remains problematic for many of the world's Muslims.

The Third Islamic Congress was held in Jerusalem in 1931, but this time the burning issue was the situation regarding the Muslims of Palestine and the protection of Islam's Holy Places in the city of Jerusalem. This took place amid escalating resentment against what were seen as pro-Zionist policies by the British government in

Palestine. The colonial juggling of France in North Africa and Italy in Libya were also condemned in no uncertain terms by the Congress—these desperate last-act scramblings for overseas territories were viewed in many respects as untamed and unnecessary acts of aggression against Islam.

In the meantime, when it came to the urgent issue of deciding what form of government was appropriate in what would become the post-colonial world, the response ranged from outright secularism to calls for the implementation of Sharia law and the full Islamization of state and society. As with the related issue of the Caliphate, there was no consensus in sight.

Secularism Versus the Islamic State

In the same country where the Caliphate had been abolished, secularism was adopted in a dramatic fashion under the leadership of the highly charismatic Kemal Ataturk, who became president of Turkey in 1923. Ataturk's sweeping reforms struck at the heart of the religious establishment. Not only did he end the Caliphate but he suppressed religious orders, replaced the Arabic alphabet with the Latin alphabet, and replaced Sharia law with the Swiss civil code. He outlawed polygamy (Muslim men are permitted to take more than one wife under certain conditions), made only civil and not religious marriages valid in the eyes of the state, and discouraged, although he did not ban, the use of the veil.

In most other Islamic states, however, governments attempted to accommodate religion to varying degrees in the turbulent years between the 1930s and 1960s. Still, the tensions that arose, even under the most traditional of transitions such as in Saudi Arabia, still have not been resolved, exacerbated by the pointed failure today of post-independent nationalist governments to deliver on promises of economic security and political equality.

Numerous Islamic movements began to flourish, and soon lined up behind the Ulema who now turned their criticism squarely on their leaders and the secular model they defended—a system critics claimed to be far from neutral but in fact a disguised package of Western values.

Governments were up against a formidable opponent. In Muslim countries the religious establishment counted on widespread popular support. The mosque provided the major focus for the community, yet it was more than just a prayer hall. It was a place of discussion and learning. Some of the most famous mosques in Islam were home to enormously influential *madrasa* schools as illustrious as any centers of learning in the West. These religious institutions also held an important charitable function, providing the social safety net when the state failed, and it was also here that educational opportunities for the poor and dispossessed were to be found.

Thus, with much of the Islamic world languishing in poverty, suffering from a pervasive malaise of disunity, and often ruled by moderate to severely repressive regimes that hid behind a thin veneer of democracy, the religious establishment became a major channel through which popular disenchantment was expressed. Indeed, in many cases, it was the only channel.

The spiral of mutual suspicion continued. In their attempts to curb opposition, governments often responded by cracking down on the burgeoning Islamic movements, censoring their publications and excluding them from the decision-making process. Driven underground, a highly extremist form of Islam was encouraged, drawing its life force from the poorest sections of the population whose needs had been ignored by their governments. This was a failure of dialogue between government and people that came to play a direct role in the massive increase of Islamic opposition groups that were to spread throughout the Middle East and in the Arab Muslim world.

The Muslim Brotherhood

Opposition to secularism in the twentieth century found its most vocal expression in the organization known as the Muslim Brotherhood. The movement was founded in 1928 in Egypt at the time that the country was struggling to gain full independence from Britain. Its founder Hassan al-Banna (1906-1949) was vociferously opposed to the West's interference not only in Egypt but in the Muslim world at large, and his goal was the establishment of Islamic states. Called in Arabic *Al-Ikhwan al-Muslimun*, or simply *Al-Ikhwan*, the Brotherhood rapidly expanded outside Egypt, spreading the philosophy that Islam is "Creed and state, book and sword, and a way of life."

A leading thinker in Al-Banna's Brotherhood was Sayyid Qutb (1906-1966), who utterly rejected the legitimacy of any government not based on the Sharia. In 1954, when the Muslim Brotherhood was banned in Egypt, Qutb, along with other members of the movement, was thrown into jail. Dubbed the "intellectual father of Islamic fundamentalism," he argued that Islam was universal in scope, applicable to everyone (Muslims and non-Muslims of any color or background) everywhere, at all times. (Interestingly, the word "fundamentalism" has its origins in the United States where it was used to describe Protestants who adhered strictly to the Scriptures.) It was, he contended, the only system that could provide solutions for the dilemmas of the modern world.

He was not looking to undo history, but saw Islam as having a profoundly beneficial role in guiding the world through the difficulties of economic development, providing an answer that world ideologies such as communism and capitalism had failed to provide. It was also Qutb who put forward the controversial justification for attacking people and property if they committed actions that were incompatible with the Islamic faith.

Qutb was a prolific writer. His best works, however, were produced after his sudden return in 1950—his opinions even more crystalized than before—from the United States, where he had gone to complete his academic studies. What disappointed him most there, he said, was the infatuation of American society with materialism and widespread "sexual anarchy." He could have gone on to study for his doctoral thesis, but decided instead to return to Egypt and devote his life to the Islamic movement.

His *Ma'alim fi 'l-Tariq* ("Milestones") is a best seller, and is said to have been published in close to 2,000 editions, but most of Qutb's books no longer can be ordered at bookstores. In recent times, they were banned by Egyptian President Hosni Mubarak. However, millions of pirated copies are being distributed through Islamic religious associations, in Europe as well as in Islamic nations.

Qutb's later theme became his prognosis that the Western, secularized world, which is deeply inferior to Islam, must be replaced by an Islamic world order. "After the complete breakdown of democracy, Western civilization has nothing else to give humanity. The dominance of Western man has reached its end. The time has come for Islam to take the lead."

Wahhabism

The West and its secular approach to government found many critics in the Islamic world, some of whom argued that the way forward in the modern world lay in reviving and promoting the values of Islam in their purest form. The trend known as Islamic Revival found its expression in movements influenced by the forceful ideas of Muhammad ibn Abd al-Wahhabi (c. 1703–1791), who was active in Arabia during the eighteenth century, a time when the Islamic world was in decline.

He was the founder of an influential Islamic revival movement which openly challenged the Ottoman authorities who claimed, although they never quite managed it, to rule over the Arabian Peninsula. Wahhabi held that Islam had lost its way. In his view, layer after layer of political and cultural impurities had been added to it over the course of the centuries and the task now was to strip these away and return to the essence of the religion. Legitimate Sunni Islamic law, he said, could only be derived from the Qur'an and Hadiths.

Puritanical in outlook, Wahhabi's followers therefore adhered to a strict interpretation of Islam and were forbidden to indulge in things such as tobacco or music. The sect also was hostile to Sufi ideas and practices and particularly discouraged the veneration of saints and pilgrimages to their tombs.

Wahhabi's ideas have had a great influence on Islamic movements elsewhere in the world including in India, Sudan, and especially Saudi Arabia. It was Wahhabi who converted the Saudi tribe in the Nejd (Central Arabia) in the middle of the eighteenth century to his brand of Islam. By 1811, the Wahhabis had managed to overrun most of Arabia, ruling it from their capital of Riyadh in the center of the peninsula. Suffering a major defeat at the hands of the Ottomans in alliance with Muhammad Ali of Egypt in 1818, the Saudi tribe nevertheless retained a varying degree of influence in the region. Their fortunes changed in the early twentieth century under the campaigns of King Ibn Saud, who consolidated Wahhabi hold over much of the peninsula, including Mecca and Medina, and founded modern Saudi Arabia in 1932.

The Wahhabi influence can be seen in the strict form of Islam found in Saudi Arabia. In recent years, however, there has been a tendency both by the West and other Islamic nations to use "Wahhabism" as a catch-all label for any extremist movement or act of terrorism that operates under the banner of Islam. The link comes mainly from the fact that Saudi Arabia funds foreign students to study in its institutions as well as having a program for building new mosques and foundations in other Muslim states. Unsurprisingly, many of the students and those associated with the mosques share Saudi religious ideals and are treated with some suspicion by their fellow countrymen. "Wahhabi" has therefore been readily applied to Muslim agents of conflict regardless of their true background or motives. The fact that experts in the West also use this epithet as a catch-all is highly misleading and unfortunate.

Yet Qutb also had a stark warning for the society in which he lived. Not only did he use the term *jahiliyya* (the state of decadence and ignorance of the type that had existed in Arabia prior to the revelation of the Quran to Muhammad) to describe state of affairs in the Capitalist and Communist worlds, he also argued that *jahiliyya* had infected the Islamic world too. During his trial at the hands of the Nasser regime he declared: "We are the *Umma* [community] of Believers, living within a society that is in a state of *jahiliyya*. Nothing relates us to the state or society and we owe no allegiance to either. As a community of believers we should see ourselves in a state of war with the State and society."

Qutb was sentenced to death and executed in 1966, accused by the government of treason. The Muslim Brotherhood has continued to thrive as an underground movement. Gaining enormous influence both in Egypt and in other countries such as Syria and Sudan, it became linked to terrorism and assassinations (although it would be wholly wrong suggest all its members are connected to terrorism). A famous offshoot of the Muslim Brotherhood is Hamas (Islamic Resistance Movement), the Palestinian extremist organization established in 1987 that has been responsible for numerous terrorist attacks against Israel.

Muslim Opposition to Israel

Few issues within the Islamic world have stirred up quite so much emotion as the fate of the Palestinians. It is a tragic situation that arose from complex historical factors that still haunt the Middle East and the rest of the world.

Palestine, once part of the now defunct Ottoman Empire, officially came under British administration in 1922 after a mandate was issued by the League of Nations in the chaotic aftermath of World War I. The region had been the focus of the Zionist movement, which had gained widespread popularity in Europe during the 1890s, and which championed the right of the homeless Jewish nation, continually faced with anti-Semitism, to establish a permanent state in Palestine.

It was a cause that the Arabs in Palestine and elsewhere thoroughly opposed. In the 1920s the Jewish community in Palestine was in a minority, accounting for some seven percent of the population, the rest being mostly Arabic-speaking Muslims, but with significant numbers of Arab Christians.

In exchange for support from the Arabs during World War I, Britain had promised to support the creation of Arab states following the fall of the Ottoman Empire, and the Arabs believed this to include Palestine—a claim denied later by the British. However, in 1917, Britain expressed its sympathy for the Jewish cause in a document known as the Balfour Declaration.

The arrival of Jewish immigrants in the region sparked off a series of riots in Palestine during the 1920s. The problem intensified after the rise of Hitler in Germany in 1933. Barred from entering other European countries, Jewish immigrants fleeing the Nazis began to flood into Palestine. Tensions mounted and, in 1936, the Arabs staged a full-scale revolt. In an attempt to solve the problem, Britain announced a proposal to partition Palestine between the Arabs and Jews. The Arabs rejected the idea outright, leaving the British to struggle in vain to come up with a workable solution to the problem.

In the aftermath of World War II, which had seen the systematic murder by the Nazis of an estimated six million European Jews, the flood of immigrants to Palestine increased manyfold. The Arab world, spurred on by its opposition to a Jewish state and its need to foster unity among its ranks, created a new organization called the League of Arab States (or the Arab League). Established in Cairo in 1945, its earliest members were Arab countries in the Middle East, including Egypt, Syria, and Transjordan (from 1949 onwards called Jordan), but it later expanded to include many other states.

With tensions between the Arabs and Jews at a breaking point, the British government washed its hands of the affair and declared in February 1947 that it had "no power to award the country either to the Arabs or the Jews, or even to partition it between them." Instead, it turned the matter over to the newly-established United Nations to find a solution.

The U.N. was faced with a formidable challenge. The Arabs rejected the partition of Palestine, favoring instead the creation of a single state with the guarantee of equal representation of Muslim, Jewish, and Christian communities alike. On the other hand, the Jews favored the creation of two separate states. The United Nations opted for partition. The region descended into a spiral of violence committed by terrorists on both sides, and before the U.N. plan could be implemented in a peaceful manner the Jews took matters into their own hands and announced the birth of the state of Israel.

The creation of Israel was met with anger across the Arab and wider Muslim world, which refused to accept the new state as having any legitimacy. An Arab attempt led by Egypt to topple Israel led to defeat. By the time a U.N.-sponsored ceasefire had been declared a month later, Israel emerged with about one-third more land than envisaged by the U.N. partition plan, including half of Jerusalem. An immediate effect of the conflict was the displacement of hundreds of thousands of Arab Palestinians. Moving into the Gaza Strip and neighboring Arab countries, they turned desperately to the U.N. for humanitarian aid. The fate of the Palestinians galvanized Muslim opinion. As the Palestinians moved out, Jewish immigrants flooded into Israel, doubling the Jewish population of the country over the next three years.

Despite the ceasefire there was no real peace. Two wars between Israel and an Arab coalition led by Egypt broke out in the following two decades, both of which were seen as humiliating defeats for Muslims. The Six-Day War fought in 1967 saw Israel gain substantial territories including Egypt's Sinai Peninsula, the West Bank, and the Golan Heights of the River Jordan. The Yom Kippur War of 1973 once again ultimately gave Israel a victory.

Egypt and Israel eventually made peace with each other after signing the Camp David Accords in Washington in 1979. While the effort had already won the Egyptian and Israelis premiers, Anwar al-Sadat and Menachim Begin, the 1978 Nobel Peace Prize, there was a pointed failure to find a solution to the Palestinian question. Sadat's rapprochement with Israel was viewed in a poor light in the Arab world and Egypt was suspended from the Arab League, whose headquarters were transferred from Cairo to Tunisia.

Sadat himself paid the ultimate price for incurring the displeasure of Islamic extremist groups. In the spirit of Qutb, the president was viewed as little better than an apostate for making peace with Israel and implementing laws that were incompatible with the Sharia and led to the suffering of Muslims. Indeed, the leader of Munazzamat al-Jihad, the group responsible for Sadat's assassination, issued a *fatwa* denouncing him as a unbeliever. Sadat was killed in a hail of bullets in 1981 while reviewing a military parade commemorating the 1973 Yom Kippur War.

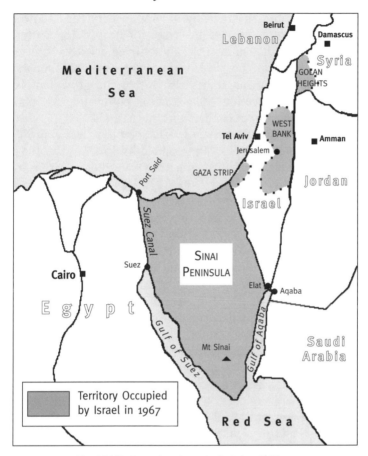

The Middle East after the 1967 Arab-Israeli War.

Inaction of the West Fuels the Palestinian Intifada

Despite the strong underlying Arab nationalist motives opposing the creation of Israel, religion remained a key issue in the Palestinian crisis. For Muslims the world over, Jerusalem and the Dome of the Rock lies within their Holy Land too—the Islamic name for Jerusalem is "Al-Quds," "the Holy City"—and millions of Muslims now find it difficult to make their pilgrimage there.

This, coupled with the continued plight of large numbers of Palestinians—Muslim and Christian—living in U.N.-supervised refugee camps and mostly without employment, has allowed the Palestinian cause to transcend traditional disputes within the international Islamic community. The rallying cry it has created has become so powerful that it has not only generated unparalleled solidarity worldwide, but it has also fueled the growth of Islamic extremist groups pursuing other radical political goals that have brought them into direct conflict with the West

Although the Sinai Peninsula was handed back to Egypt in 1982, the increasing settlement of lands gained by Israel in the 1967 War and its often heavy-handed treatment of Palestinians within its new borders saw the eruption in 1987 of the Palestinian "Intifada" or "Uprising." Over the next few years, the Palestinians waged a campaign of open revolt against the Israeli authorities.

Hope came in the 1990s with international peace initiatives, beginning with the Oslo Agreement, signed between the Palestine Liberation Organization (P.L.O.) and Israel in Washington in 1993, which provided for the phasing in of limited autonomy within the West Bank and the Gaza Strip. It was a time that saw the P.L.O., representing most of the Palestinian people, renounce terrorism. The promise of a Palestinian state with limited powers was finally established under the leadership of the P.L.O.'s Yasser Arafat.

However, the P.L.O.'s dialogue with the state of Israel was undermined as Hamas and other other militant groups launched a sustained campaign against the Israelis, including suicide bombings. Their intention was to derail any further negotiations over the status of the new Palestine, calling for nothing less that the complete withdrawal of Israeli troops from the West Bank and Gaza Strip.

By the early 2000s any chance of peace seemed to have vanished. Key issues such as the settlements of clearly demarcated Palestinian lands by Israeli settlers and the non-fulfillment of a slew of longstanding U.N. resolutions by Israel proved a major sticking point.

The result was the unleashing of a new and far deadlier Intifada, and Israelis and Palestinians descended into a tragic spiral of violence. Terrorist attacks against Israelis led to military reprisals that were intended to paralyze the Palestinian leadership. Israel repeatedly held P.L.O. leader Yasser Arafat accountable for the violence, but many of the terrorist attacks, typified by suicide bombings, were carried out by militant groups such as Hamas and Islamic Jihad, over whom it was doubtful the beleaguered Palestinian leader had much, if any, influence. The popularity of Hamas, which promised to intensify its armed struggle against Israel, soared in the atmosphere of despair that followed the demise of the peace process.

Palestinian and Israeli moderates have worked hard for a resolution to the conflict, but the fragile process is open to constant hijacking by extremists on both sides or political expediency of the Western powers. Meanwhile, the Palestinians themselves remain trapped in the slums, ghettos, and refugee camps of a half-nation that has no real economy or the means to adequately defend it, able only to watch in frustration as the prize of full statehood remains as elusive as ever.

Islam and the West
—Facing Difficult Times

"These are tense times, but it is better to think in terms of powerful and powerless communities, the secular politics of reason and ignorance, and universal principles of justice and injustice, than to wander off in search of vast abstractions that may give momentary satisfaction but little self-knowledge or informed analysis."
—*Thinker Edward Said, writing in* The Nation, *2001*

Terrorism, suicide bombers, public beheadings, the veil and book burning—these are some of the highly emotive issues that cast a long shadow in the minds of many people over the religion of Islam during the latter part of the twentieth century and early twenty-first century. With such themes becoming the staple of Western newspapers, magazines, and television programs, attitudes in the West hardened towards Muslims, as the latter became almost a byword for intolerance and injustice.

Alarmingly, in the wake of the collapse of the Soviet Union, it appeared that in place of ideological divisions drawn up along the lines of democracy versus Communism there was a new global rift— this time one between the West and the Islamic world. Ideas put forward by both Islamic and Western thinkers maintaining that the two sides were destined to clash in a struggle that left room for only one victor began to gain ground. In the West, with a long history of suspicion towards Islam, such fears were fueled by a number of events that were held by many to be examples of the innate incompatibility of Islamic and democratic values.

Modern Islamic Revolution—Iran

Those countries which came under the scrutiny of the West were ones in which Islamic-based revolutions had taken place, notably in Iran and Afghanistan. Attacking Western values and rejecting outside interference, the new governing elites closely identified themselves with Islam and actively sought to rebuild the institutions of the state according to their own interpretations of the religion.

Prior to the Iranian revolution of 1979, Iran had been ruled by the secular regime of the Pahlavi Shahs. The regime enjoyed considerable support from the West, especially the United States, and was seen as an important barrier against Soviet encroachment in the Middle East as well as a key guardian of Western oil interests in the region. However, the last Shah faced strong opposition from the religious establishment over his secularist policies, as well as from the political left over his increasing dependency on the United States. By 1978, the country had descended into chaos and violence, and, faced with massive opposition, the following year the Shah was forced into exile. In post-revolutionary Iran, it was the Shi'i religious establishment that finally seized power, headed by the highly charismatic imam, Ayatollah Khomeini, who returned from his own exile in France.

Khomeini firmly closed the door on the West, and drew up a new constitution that reflected Islamic values but at the same time showed its modern revolutionary ideological roots. The success of the revolution galvanized Islamic groups of the Middle East, who now hailed Iran as the first genuine Islamic state of the post-colonial era, seeing in it the chance of toppling the corrupt regimes of their own countries. It was also Khomeini who famously issued the *fatwa* calling for the death of the British-based Muslim writer Salman Rushdie because his novel *The Satanic Verses* was regarded as blasphemous.

The Iranian experiment went sour from the outset as the regime turned on its opponents and even supporters with excessive brutality. Furthermore, an invasion by neighboring Iraq led to a disastrous war that lasted eight years (1980-88) and left up to 1.5 million dead from both sides. After Khomeini's death in 1989, there was an attempt to introduce greater political freedom and end the country's isolation from the international community. This process was hindered both by domestic opposition and blockades imposed by the West. Disenchantment with the regime, however, was never far from the surface, as witnessed in 2003 when significant numbers of students risked punishment by staging public protests calling for more freedom and democracy, yet another impassioned plea demonstrating the will and desire of Muslims to create the conditions to solve their own problems.

The Taliban

The Islamic revolution that gained the most notoriety in the West was that staged by the Taliban in Afghanistan in the mid-1990s. The regime's policies and imposition of Islamic law based on an uncompromising and highly questionable interpretation of Sharia law received heavy media coverage in the West, doing much to convince America and Europe that the realization of an Islamic state could bring little else but medieval barbarity.

The Taliban were a group of students whose sudden rise to leadership had taken place amidst the chaos into which the country had descended after fourteen terrible years of civil war, accompanied by invasion on the part of the Soviet Union—a disastrous undertaking that has been likened to a kind of "Soviet Vietnam." A Taliban spokesman, Mullah Wakil Ahmed, quoted in 1996 by the Arabic magazine *Al-Majalla*, described the conditions under which his movement came about:

> After the Mojahedin parties [the Taliban's predecessors] came to power in 1992, the Afghan people thought that peace would prevail in the country. However, the leaders began to fight over power in Kabul. Some local leaders, particularly in Kandahar, formed armed gangs that fought each other. There was widespread corruption and theft, and there were roadblocks everywhere. Women were being attacked, raped, and killed. Therefore, after these incidents, a group of students from religious schools decided to rise against these leaders in order to alleviate the suffering of the residents of Kandahar Province.

Seizing power over most, but not all of Afghanistan, the Taliban set about establishing a new state based on Sharia law. According to their strict interpretation of Islam, a whole range of restrictions and bans were introduced. Many of these were not prescribed by the Qur'an. In public, women were forced to wear the all-enveloping black *burqas*, intended to cover every inch of their bodies, and required to be escorted by a close male relative—in some cases making the simple act of leaving the house impossible. Failure to comply would most likely be met with physical blows from police armed with sticks. The *Hudud* laws (governing morality, including matters of dress, adultery, theft, and even television-watching in Afghanistan) prescribed punishments such as amputation of hands for robbery and public stoning or shootings for adultery. Women were not allowed to work under the Taliban, although a lifting of the injunction was not ruled out once stability had been established. Men were forced to grow beards, in emulation of Muhammad who always wore one, and were banned from wearing Western clothes.

Yet the Taliban leadership had no doubt that they were upholding the values of Islam and announced on their Voice of Sharia Radio station in 1994:

> By the enforcement of the Sharia *Hudud* we have made safe the lives and property of millions of people from Herat to Jalalabad and Kabul. No one can commit theft or crimes. We have not introduced this law. This is the law that was revealed by God to Muhammad. Those who consider the imposition of this law to be against human rights are insulting all Muslims and their beliefs.

Of course, the Taliban (who were mostly Pashtuns, one of the major Afghan ethnic groups, and who were educated in fundamentalist *madrasas* in refugee camps in neighboring Pakistan) were not imposing Islam on their country. They were in fact imposing a set of rules and a political ideology legitimized by a very narrow interpretation of Islam on an ethnically diverse population that was indeed already Muslim.

The Afghans had a long tradition of Islam and had little need to be guided in their faith by a group such as the Taliban. In their zealotry the Taliban even attempted to eradicate all traces of the region's rich non-Islamic past and decreed in February, 2002, that "all the statues in the country should be destroyed because they have been used as idols and deities by nonbelievers before."

Dramatically putting words into practice, the regime subsequently blew up the two famed giant Buddha statues hewn into a rock face in Bamyan, central Afghanistan. The statues, which dated from the third and fifth centuries A.D., were considered to be among the finest

The Veil—Islamic or Cultural Practice?

A potent symbol used to highlight the intolerance and incompatibility of Islam with modern Western values is the veil. The issue became especially pronounced during the 1990s with the rule of the Taliban, in Afghanistan. Images of women wearing *burqas*, cloaklike coverings stretching from head to foot designed to hide their faces and bodies, were seen as synonymous with Islam, which apparently cared little for women's rights or dignity and made them invisible in society—a shocking example of woman's enforced subordination to unchecked male domination.

It is interesting to note that some forty years before the Taliban regime, in an attempt to encourage women to appear in public with their faces uncovered, the prime minister of the very same country, himself a Muslim, challenged his critics among the Ulema (who feared that Islamic standards were being eroded by Soviet influences) to find indisputable evidence in the Islamic canonical law, the Sharia, to justify the need to veil the face. They were not able to do this.

In fact, the use of the veil is not exclusive to Islam and, far from being a Muslim invention, predates the religion. The practice of women hiding their faces and largely living in seclusion appeared in Classical Greece, in the Byzantine Christian world, in Persia, and in India among upper-caste Rajput women. The problem the Ulema in Afghanistan encountered was that there is no specific ruling on the matter of veiling in the Qur'an, merely guidance on modesty. While women are instructed to look away from temptation and to "draw their veils over their bosoms," there is no instruction to veil their faces so that they may not be seen. Within the Hadiths too, there is no clear-cut answer although many of today's practices are based on their example.

The matter of veiling, as is the case with other issues concerning women in the Muslim communities of the world, highlights the complexities arising from the fact that the Islamic world covers an extensive portion of the globe and a great many different cultures. The cultural norm for Muslims in one region may be taboo for those Muslims in another region.

The term "veiling" also causes some confusion since it is often used to refer to scarves that do not in fact cover the face. Traditional dress codes in fact vary sharply in different Muslim societies and a variety of different styles of head and face coverings exist. The all-enveloping *burqa*, worn particularly in Africa and the Middle East, has gained a great deal of notoriety in the West. In Iran, the black *chador*, a more flexible body covering, is traditional among wide sectors of society but, according to the occasion, many women there tend to wear the *hijab*, worn also by American Muslim women in the form of large scarves that cover their hair, neck, and sometimes shoulders. In Muslim areas of Southeast Asia, women wear scarves that cover their hair but leave their faces visible. Nomadic Bedouin women of the Arabian Peninsula wear the same—just like most of their men—but in this case they are combining modesty with vital protection against the sun and harsh desert climate.

Certainly in the early days of the Arab Empire, the idea of veiling was far from accepted by all women, and during the first century the matter of female dress was somewhat more relaxed. It is said that after the son of a prominent Companion of the Prophet Muhammad asked his wife to veil her face, she refused, replying: "Since God Almighty has sealed me with the stamp of beauty, I desire that He should behold it and recognize His grace towards them, and I will not veil it. Verily, there is no defect in me, that anyone should speak of it."

The thinker Qasim Amin (1865-1908) is firmly linked with the movement for women's emancipation in Egypt in the first part of the twentieth century. After completing legal studies in France in 1885, Amin returned to Egypt where he served as a judge and participated in the founding of Cairo University. He called for a radical reappraisal of women's rights within Islam and criticized the wearing of the veil as a cultural practice, not an Islamic one.

Amid the debate he caused came some surprising countercriticisms from a female perspective, notably from the famed fellow Egyptian writer Malak Hifni Nassef (1886-1918). Taking issue with yet more dictates from men, she declared against Muslim men in general: "If he orders us to veil, we veil, and if he now demands that we unveil, we unveil. There is no doubt that he has erred grievously against us in decreeing our rights in the past and no doubt that he errs grievously in decreeing our rights now." Arguing for greater education and a change in the culture of male-dominated Egyptian society of her day, Nassef emphasized that before women could go unveiled, it would be necessary for men to learn not to harass women who were unveiled. This is still the attitude in many Islamic countries.

According to Islamic thought, the veil is a symbol of more than physical covering. Crucially, it is part of a concept of modesty that applies to every aspect of behavior, manners, speech and appearance in public. Dress is merely one facet of the total being—and the basic requirements of clothing for a Muslim female apply equally to those of a Muslim male, with the difference being mainly in degree.

The writer and thinker Fatima Mernissi views the recent rise of enforced veiling and women's repression in some Muslim countries as a rejection of Western, colonial influence. As she says in her book *Beyond the Veil: Male-Female Dynamics in Modern Muslim Society*: "The fact that Western colonizers took over the paternalistic defense of the Muslim woman's lot characterized any changes in her condition as concessions to the colonizer. Since the external aspects of women's liberation, for example, the neglect of the veil for Western dress, were often emulations of Western women, women's liberation was readily identified as succumbing to foreign influences." This sheds light on recent events like the reinstitution of mandatory veiling by Afghanistan's Taliban regime.

examples of art of that period, and their destruction caused international uproar—not merely in non-Muslim countries. Neighboring Iran, for example, condemned the act as an assault on the "country's cultural and national heritage [which belonged] to the history of the region's civilization in which all humanity has a share." (Ironically, in the eighteenth century, during a military campaign, the Persian ruler Nadir Shah ordered the faces of the statues to be sawn off.)

The Taliban were far from representing the Afghans as a whole, a people that by and large have been proud of their non-Islamic heritage, one which famously includes the marriage of Alexander the Great to one of their princesses, Roxana—an event that opened the country up to Ancient Greek influence. After the introduction of Islam, the peoples of Afghanistan gave the world some of the most enlightened examples of Islamic culture.

The Taliban's hold on the ravaged country was precarious at best and at the same time that the regime was engaged in a bloody civil war, in the territory under its control it ruthlessly crushed the smallest signs of dissent, just like its predecessors. It was an experiment that showed signs of ultimately being unworkable, wedded as it was to a highly flawed and idiosyncratic form of Islam.

But the Taliban regime had unwittingly expedited its own early demise by setting itself on a collision course with the West. While its leadership had not aimed to export its own brand of Islam—its key concern was the immense task of imposing its authority in an Afghanistan already splintered by decades of war, civil war, and occupation—it had allowed the mastermind of one of the most ruthless international terrorist organizations, Osama bin Laden, to settle in Afghanistan. There he presided over the running of military training camps for his followers, known collectively as Al-Qaeda. Consequently, Afghanistan would prove to be the first major battlefield in the U.S.-led coalition mobilized to fight international terrorism perpetrated by the ever-growing numbers of Islamic extremist organizations.

Al Qaeda and September 11

As we have seen, the West's support of Israel and its perceived lack of will to help resolve the Palestinian issue had placed it in the line of fire of extremist Islamic organizations. Terrorist attacks on Western targets during the 1990s intensified alarmingly. Furthermore, the West had clashed head on with Muslim opinion during the 1990 Gulf War, in which a U.S.-led coalition liberated Kuwait from an Iraq invasion ordered by Iraq's president Saddam Hussein.

Issues such as these, together with Western backing of unpopular governments in the Islamic world contributed to making the United States and its allies direct targets of Muslim extremists. Claiming their cause transcended national borders and the promotion of particular existing states, Bin Laden and Al-Qaeda appealed to the *Umma*, the international community of Islam, and in so doing created a highly charged political and religious ideology.

Bin Laden's own particular bitterness was directed towards the Saud family that ruled over Saudi Arabia—or what Bin Laden preferred to call the "Land of the Two Holy Mosques" (Mecca and Medina). For Bin Laden, a wealthy Saudi citizen of Yemeni origin, Saudi Arabia was an entity lacking any legitimacy. A key aim behind his meticulous campaign of terrorism, which proved so damaging to relations between Islam and the West, was to see the removal of American military bases from Saudi Arabia.

To these ends, Bin Laden drew on the support of opponents of the hugely wealthy Saud family and their tight hold on power. Bin Laden tapped into a source of ready-made popular support by identifying his organization with the Palestinian cause in Israel and with opposition to the Western powers that shored up both Israel and Saudi Arabia. Ironically, the West also covertly supported extremist Islamic groups acting against regimes considered to be against Western interests—and nowhere is this more highlighted than by the C.I.A.'s funding and training of Osama bin Laden as a destabilizing agent during the war between Afghanistan and the Soviet Union in the 1980s.

Expertly generating a wealth of funds over the years through the international stock markets, Al-Qaeda's carefully orchestrated waves of terror attacks culminated in an atrocity that earned the organization a place in the annals of world notoriety—that of September 11, 2001. On that day, nineteen terrorists hijacked four passenger planes, flying two of them into the Twin Towers of the World Trade Center in New York City and another into the Pentagon in Washington—the fourth crashed in the countryside in Pennsylvania. The death toll was estimated to be around three thousand, which included a significant number of Muslims.

When it became apparent that Al-Qaeda and Bin Laden were responsible, a worldwide campaign was launched to apprehend the perpetrators, which included a dramatic U.S.-led invasion of Afghanistan, where Al-Qaeda was based. There, only two days before September 11, suicide bombers from Al-Qaeda had killed Ahmed Shah Masoud, head of the anti-Taliban opposition. While the U.S. military operation failed to capture Bin Laden and see an end to Al-Qaeda, it resulted in the toppling of the Taliban government in 2001, its demise mourned by few, but offering few answers to restoring stability to Afghanistan.

Muslim Condemnation of September 11

Al-Qaeda and Bin Laden undeniably attracted popular support from certain sections of the Islamic world. In poor neighborhoods around the Islamic world, Bin Laden T-shirts and other merchandise sporting the Al-Qaeda leader's image became popular. Enjoying a carefully cultivated personality cult akin to the one that grew around the similarly defective (and politically rejected) Che Guevara of the Cuban Revolution, he was held to be a folk hero fighting the oppressive regimes in the Muslim world that kept people like themselves poor and powerless. Yet the many clear condemnations against those who committed the atrocities, issued by scores of local and international Muslim leaders, scholars, and organizations, were overlooked in the Western press—as had regularly been the case in previous terrorist attacks.

With their numerous statements issued immediately after the tragedy, Muslims the world over not only expressed their sympathies for the victims but also made clear that from an Islamic point of view the attacks were indefensible. In the days following the attacks, more than a hundred major Islamic movements from numerous countries issued a joint declaration "unequivocally" condemning the attack as:

> . . . a crime against all humanity, and Muslims all over the world mourn all the victims of this aggression as a common loss of America and the whole world. We also affirm that victims of terrorism in all parts of the world deserve equal sympathy and concern, and all those who stand for the equality

of humankind must condemn and fight terrorism in all parts of the world. We also uphold and affirm the principle that whoever is responsible for acts of terrorism against human beings—individual, group or government—must be brought to justice and punished for that without discrimination.

In the United States, Muslim scholars were unanimous in their condemnation. The Sharia Scholars Association of North America declared it an "immoral and inhumane act," while Shaikh Muhammad Hanooti of the Fiqh Council of North America reiterated that "Islam tells us that murdering one person is equal to murdering all humanity." In the United Kingdom, following a conference held on September 29, the Muslim Council of Britain issued a written statement condemning "absolutely" the atrocities, affirming that "the killing of innocent people, whether done by individuals, groups, organizations, or state institutions, is condemned in Islam."

On September 18, Dr. Tahir ul Qadri, founder of the Minhaj-ul-Qur'an movement of Pakistan, publicly declared on Pakistan TV that:

> Terrorism is not allowed in Islam. It is totally against Islam to kill non-combatants, women, minors. Just killing people [indiscriminately] is not jihad and is against the spirit of Islam . . . people must understand that terrorism and jihad are two different things.

A few days later, on September 24, at the famed Al-Azhar Mosque and University in Cairo, the Grand Imam, Shaikh Mohamed Sayed Tantawi, denounced the act as "mean and hideous," adding that:

> . . . attacking innocent people is not courageous and will be punished on the Day of Judgment. It is not courageous to attack innocent children, women, and civilians.

Reactions to the International War against Terrorism

While the September 11 attacks attracted strong condemnation from the Islamic world, the U.S.-led response, which saw the launch of an international war against terrorism, caused great disquiet among Muslims. The Western coalition took a great deal of care to highlight the campaign as not targeted against Muslims, but against terrorists pursuing an agenda shaped by a political ideology that exploited Islam for their own ends. However, the chosen strategy to tackle the threat involved physically setting foot in Muslim countries. The subsequent military operations were seen as alarmingly reminiscent of the days of Western colonialism from which Muslims had struggled so hard to free themselves. Muslim critics warned of a worrying new and aggressive form of Western imperialism. Meanwhile, governments in Islamic countries that had been persuaded to allow Western forces on their territory or that had initiated anti-terrorist operations were left open to the criticism of either dancing to the tune of the West, or of using the situation as a pretext for cracking down on domestic opposition.

Thus, Muslims were deeply affected by the Western invasions of Afghanistan in 2001 and Iraq in 2003. The question of Iraq was particularly thorny given that few were convinced that there was any connection between the government of Saddam Hussein and Al-Qaeda. Equally problematic was the inability of international observers and weapons inspectors to ascertain the extent to which the country contributed to international terrorism or posed a threat to the region. Such unease was also widely felt in Western countries where millions of non-Muslims marched alongside Muslims to voice their concerns—Britain, for example, saw the biggest peace protest it had ever experienced when a million people from across the political and religious spectrum brought the streets of central London to a standstill.

Saddam Hussein's regime was, in fact, of a secular nature and poles opposite to that of the Taliban—by all accounts his true hero was Joseph Stalin, head of the Soviet Union. All in all, it was exactly the kind of regime Osama bin Laden had sworn to overthrow. Indeed, prior to the 1991 Gulf War, sparked off by Iraq's invasion of Kuwait, Saddam Hussein had been the head of just one of a string of unpopular regimes propped up by the West. (It was only the dictator's miscalculation that he could invade and keep Kuwait in 1991 that put him permanently on the wrong side of his Western benefactors.)

After the Gulf War, Saddam Hussein attempted to play the religious card, but it was a performance that convinced few. The Ulema, along with almost every other section of society in Iraq, was heavily repressed. Saddam Hussein and his ruling clan were, in fact,

The Nation of Islam

In America, Islam found an unusual and highly controversial advocate in the form of an African-American preacher by the name of Wallace Fard Muhammad. In the early 1930s, during the Great Depression, Fard devoted his considerable energies to traveling in the Midwest and bringing a '"racialized" variant of Islam to black communities there. African Americans, he declared, were really Muslims who had been separated from their original Islamic roots.

Fard disappeared in 1934—it is believed to Mecca—and his torch was carried by his follower Elijah Muhammad (born Elijah Poole 1897). A one-time Baptist minister, Elijah Muhammad hailed his teacher as a Mahdi, and went on to found the Nation of Islam which he would head until his death in 1975. Muhammad claimed to be a prophet appointed by Fard to spread his word. The Nation of Islam (N.O.I.) addressed the issue of race and religion by stating that it was the destiny of the black race, the descendants of God, to reclaim the planet after a period of international strife. The new religion threw back at the white community many of the myths and derogatory views that had been forced on black people. A strong moral code meant that followers were banned from using alcohol, tobacco or any other kinds of drugs, as well as prohibited from participating in activities such as gambling and dancing. Western names were replaced with Muslim names, which represented a casting aside of slave names and embracing the new Muslim identity.

In fact, key N.O.I. beliefs ran counter to the core values of Islam, not least the doctrine of racial exclusiveness—a fact that would become apparent to one of its best-known members, Malcolm X (1925-1965), whose views softened after making the pilgrimage to Mecca where he witnessed the startling ethnic diversity united in one faith (he subsequently converted to Sunni Islam).

After Elijah Muhammad's death in 1975, his son Wallace took over the leadership of the N.O.I. The movement underwent a transformation as Wallace renamed it the American Muslim Mission, cast off its racist doctrine and brought it more in line with orthodox (Sunni) Islam.

However, a branch of the N.O.I., led by Louis Farrakhan, attempted to revive the original doctrines of racial separation. Farrakhan subsequently attempted to diffuse his more radical policies, culminating in the Million Man March, following his call for a "Day of Atonement" that would focus attention on the social and economic problems plaguing African-American males. On October 16, 1995, hundreds of thousands of African-American men congregated in Washington, D.C., to hear speeches from black luminaries such as Rosa Parks, Jesse Jackson, and Maya Angelou. In his address Farrakhan urged black men to take responsibility for themselves, their families, their communities, and America itself, instead of blaming their conditions on outside forces. Primarily organized by former National Association for the Advancement of Colored People (N.A.A.C.P.) executive director Benjamin Chavis, it was the single largest gathering of African-Americans in history.

Sunnis, and the Shi'is, who comprise the majority of the Iraqi population, found their political and religious expression severely curtailed. The major Shi'i pilgrimage to Karbala in honor of Imam Hussein's martyrdom in A.D. 680, was banned in 1977, a year in which Saddam Hussein's forces slaughtered many pilgrims making their way to the city. Thousands of students and teachers and a number of key Shi'i ayatollahs, or religious leaders, at the seminary in Najaf (an important shrine city) were executed or put in prison by the regime. Such acts provoked two failed Shi'i revolts in 1990s. It was estimated that the number of ayatollahs in Najaf during three decades leading up to the fall of Saddam Hussein dropped from more than 7,000 to fewer than 1,750, which inflicted a severe blow to the seminary.

It was telling that on the downfall of Saddam Hussein's regime, Iraqi voices were heard to question why it was the West and not the Arab nations that had toppled such a tyrant—a sign of the lack of unity and powerless of the Arab and wider Islamic world. Whatever the complexities of the 2003 war, Muslim deaths at the hands of Western soldiers shocked the Muslim world. The lack of any clear commitment by the West to bring lasting peace to the Middle East, including its failure to push ahead with a Palestinian solution, left the key reasons for the invasion of Iraq unresolved. This also has done little to dispel suspicions that more Muslim countries would be open to attack by the West, more likely motivated by concerns over access to oil and strategic control than humanitarian concerns.

Muslims as Victims

The reality is that Muslims are just as likely as non-Muslims, if not more, to become victims of Islamic extremism. Even where terrorist groups specifically target Westerners, they have increasingly shown a tendency to take little heed of Muslim lives, as the bombings that took place in cities in Saudi Arabia and Morocco in May 2003 amply testify. Other bombings by Islamic groups in Bali, Kenya, and Tanzania hit Westerners, Muslims, and other non-Westerners alike.

It is apparent that even if the West was no longer in the equation, terrorists such as Al-Qaeda, who have clearly shown their readiness to kill Muslims, might well turn their attention subsequently to those Muslims who were prepared to oppose their particular extreme and uncompromising views, not least those who lean towards secularism.

The fact that many Muslims have undoubtedly thrived within the secular business-orientated world is evidenced by countries such as Indonesia and by those millions who have emigrated to Western countries and established successful businesses or boosted the ranks of the key professions. It has also been held by some that terrorist attacks involving Western targets are better explained as not an attack on the West itself, but part of a wider struggle in the Muslim world, especially Saudi Arabia, to stem the movement towards greater Islamic pluralism by growing middle classes that have the advantage of education and wealth, and now wish to change outmoded regimes.

It is not only bombs that cause such localized violence. The human rights situation in Algeria, for example, has been horrific, the legacy of France's botched imperialism. Thousands of men, women and children have been killed, many massacred in their own homes, both by security forces and the government-backed militias and by extremist Islamic groups. Meanwhile, in the Sudan, a terrible civil war has divided the country politically and religiously for more than twenty years and caused the displacement of an estimated five million people.

Apart from the grief caused by terrorism, another lamentable effect, and no doubt a major goal of extremists, has been the isolation of the Islamic world at a time when any opportunity to strengthen links between it and the West are paramount. As Westerners are killed or injured in Islamic countries, Western businessmen and tourists are warned to steer clear of them. As a result, each time Western embassies declare an entire Muslim country off-limits to their own nationals, it simply intensifies the climate of mutual suspicion, additionally costing these countries vital business and foreign revenues that they can ill-afford to lose. The net result is further deprivation—a potential recipe for destabilization.

Although bad press and the feeling that the West is hostile to the Muslim world are a deterrent to those Muslims that can afford to visit Western countries, the sad reality is that the poverty gap is so great that many nationals of Muslim countries could never afford such a journey except as immigrant workers. And for those Muslim communities already living within Western countries, this state of affairs has left them isolated too, and faced with alarming displays of "Islamophobia" from the wider community.

Afterword
—The Challenge
of the Future

It was not our intention to leave this history of the international Islamic community on a negative note. However, the advent of the new millennium, rather than heralding in an era of world peace, seems only to have brought more conflict with it. The lessons of history appear not to have been learned and the world seems powerless to prevent the ongoing wars, famine, and genocides taking place on every continent. As the September 11 attacks showed, even the United States, which has long held off war from its own shores, is no longer immune.

As with the rest of the global community, Muslims have been attempting to come to terms with a rapidly changing world and dealing with a range of dilemmas that strongly test their faith. Yet philosophical, ethical, and moral debates abound within every community, whether religious or not—issues relating to the rapid pace of modernity, such as the ethics of genetic engineering or the loss of traditional family values. As such, these are open debates over which the West has no monopoly and ones which ultimately can be only resolved with the full participation of all sections of our world society.

Politically, the blueprint for a sustainable modern state that merges a workable balance of Islamic and democratic values is difficult to define. Nevertheless, the overwhelming majority of Muslims will argue that their religion is not incompatible with the principles of democracy, especially the idea that the voice of the people should be heard and acted upon, and that people have the right to choose their leaders.

Muslims throughout history have excelled in forging strong links not only among themselves but also with other communities, both as a majority force and as minorities, such as those that have established themselves firmly in today's non-Muslim nations—a demonstration of the flexibility of their faith, one that supports values such as fair rules of trade, respect of contract, and private property. Furthermore, as minorities, Muslims consider it a moral duty to comply with the laws of the lands in which they live so long as they are treated with respect and permitted to practice their religion there.

Yet it would be wrong to assume that the society Muslims choose to live in would exactly mirror Western models of democracy. Holding that Islam is flexible enough to adapt to a modern technological society, many Muslim thinkers nevertheless emphasize that a system of morality derived from the Qur'an is necessary to prevent humankind from descending into an anarchic, corrupt and self-centered existence where individuals ignore any obligation of social responsibility.

Perhaps from a Muslim viewpoint the excesses of the West would indicate that truly inclusive democracy in the West is a new phenomenon, and one that is still in the process of being defined. Muslims would surely point out that this democracy was baptized by the conquests of the European colonial powers, slavery, religious persecution, and centuries of turmoil leading to the carnage of two World Wars. The West has a far from blemish-free record in its quest for liberty for all.

Meanwhile, as Muslims would also comment, recent excesses of violence committed in the Islamic world cannot be considered to be committed on behalf of fairly elected governments, but—as in cases such as Iraq's Saddam Hussein, and Afghanistan's Taliban regime—by a tyrannical elite whose main victims were exclusively their own compatriots. It is unjust to conclude from the actions of this minority that all Muslims are hostile to democracy, just as it is unjust to judge the whole Islamic World by the never-ending turbulence of the Middle East.

Perhaps the answer lies in the future, when secular, democratic nations like Turkey and Malaysia will show to one and all by example how Islam and the West are not mutually incompatible. The West in particular will have to embrace Turkey in every respect, because, already a key part of N.A.T.O. since 1952, one day it will be eligible for admittance to the fold of the European Union as the first member state to enjoy a predominately Islamic culture.

*

Key Dates in Islamic History

c.570   The Prophet Muhammad born in Mecca.

610   Muhammad receives the first of many revelations in Mecca.

622   Flight of Muhammad and his followers from Mecca to Medina (Yathrib).

624   Battle of Badr—Muslims defeat Meccans.

630   Mecca conquered by Muhammad and his Followers.

632-661 The period of rule by the four "Rightly Guided Caliphs": Abu Bakr (r. 632-34), Umar (634-44), Uthman (644-56) and Ali (656-61). Considered by Sunnis to be their Golden Age.

661   Ali assassinated. His supporters proclaim his son Hassan Caliph, but Hassan makes an agreement with Mu'awiya and declines. Umayyad rule begins under Mu'awiya. Oversees the greatest period of Muslim expansion and rules Islamic Empire from Damascus.

680   Husayn, Ali's son, massacred along with supporters at Karbala.

750   Abbasid dynasty overthrows Umayyads, and in 762 transfers Caliphate to Baghdad.

756   Independent Umayyad emirate established in Spain.

868   Ibn Tulun defies Abbasids and establishes near-independent rule in Egypt.

969   Shi'i Fatimid dynasty gains control of Egypt and becomes major rival to the Abbasids.

1055   Seljuks enter Baghdad and establish themselves as rulers, but maintain Abbasid Caliphs as religious figureheads.

1071-81 Seljuks establish Sultanate of Rum in Anatolia.

1095   The Pope in Rome preaches the need for a Holy War to liberate the Holy Land.

1096   Western Europe launches the first of several major Christian crusades in the Middle East, seizing Jerusalem and establishing Christian kingdoms.

1187   Saladin recaptures Jerusalem.

1258   Destruction of Baghdad by the Mongols under Hulegu who murder the Caliph and his family.

1260   Mamluks defeat Mongols at Ayn Jalut and establish supremacy in Egypt, Palestine, and Syria.

1293   Last of the Crusader occupation forces repelled.

1325   Ibn Battuta sets out on his travels.

1326   Ottomans establish capital at Bursa in Anatolia.

1369   Timur establishes rule from Samarkand.

1453   Ottomans seize Constantinople and consolidate Empire.

1492   Granada, last bastion of Islam in Spain, falls to the Catholic monarchy, leading to persecution and eventual expulsion of all Jews and Muslims.

1501   Persian Safavid dynasty founded by Ismail, who becomes Shah of Iran in 1502.

1516-17 Ottomans defeat Mamluks and add Egypt and Arabia, including Mecca and Medina, to Empire.

1526   Babur conquers Delhi and establishes the Mughal dynasty in India.

1529   Ottomans launch first of two unsuccessful attacks on Vienna.

1571	Battle of Lepanto—Ottomans defeated by Christian European coalition off coast of Greece.
1658	Aurangzeb (r. 1658-1707) becomes Mughal Emperor and reverses policies of his predecessors, imposing strict Muslim rule.
1683	Second failed Ottoman siege of Vienna. Ottoman fortunes begin to decline.
1722	Safavid dynasty overthrown by Afghans, repelled by Nadir Shah who eventually seizes power for himself.
1794	Qajar dynasty established in Iran, rules until 1925.
1798	France invades Egypt.
1832	Greece breaks away from Ottoman Empire.
1803-13	Wahhabis stage revolution against Ottomans in Arabia.
1805	Muhammad Ali becomes Pasha of Egypt, effectively ruling independently from Ottomans.
1813	Treaty of Gulistan: Iran relinquishes territorial claims in the Caucasus, Russia consolidates hold over region.
1839	First of three Anglo-Afghan wars.
1858	Britain formally dismantles Mughal Empire and establishes imperial rule in India.
1860s	Russia launches campaign in Central Asia and establishes control over the khanates of Khiva, Bukhara, and Turkestan.
1853	Crimean War. Ottoman Empire declares war after Russia occupies its vassal states of Moldavia and Walachia.
1882	Britain establishes military force of occupation in Egypt which remains until 1950s.
1914	Egypt made a protectorate and formally breaks with Ottoman Empire.
1917	Balfour Declaration states British support for Zionist movement aiming to establish a Jewish homeland in Palestine.
1918	Ottoman Empire formally dismantled.
1922	Palestine officially becomes British protectorate.
1923	Ataturk becomes president of modern Turkey and imposes sweeping reforms to secularize the country, abolishing the Caliphate in 1924.
1947	Partition in India leads to creation of Muslim Pakistan, leading to terrible violence between Muslims and Hindus.
1948	State of Israel created, sparking first Arab-Israeli war and leads to massive Palestinian refugee crisis.
1956	Nasser of Egypt nationalizes Suez Canal, causing British/French/Israeli invasion; U.N. condemnation leads to withdrawal of troops.
1967	Six-Day War, Israel seizes Sinai from Egypt and occupies the Golan Heights and West Bank.
1971	East Pakistan breaks away from West Pakistan and becomes Bangladesh.
1973	Yom Kippur War—Egypt military offensive to regain Sinai ultimately fails but leads to major international peace talks.
1978	Egypt and Israel make peace after signing the Camp David Accords. Egypt faces heavy criticism from Arab states and is expelled from the Arab League.
1979	Shah of Iran deposed by revolution. Ayatollah Khomeini returns from exile in Paris, and becomes Iran's new head of state.
1979	Russian troops enter Afghanistan.

Key Dates in Islamic History

1980-88	War between Iran and Iraq leads to as many as 1.5 million deaths.
1987	Intifada uprising by Palestinians begins.
1991	Gulf War: U.S. leads international coalition against Saddam Hussein and Iraq to liberate Kuwait.
1991	Collapse of Soviet Union leads to creation of five new republics with majority Sunni Muslim populations in Central Asia, and Republic of Azerbaijan in the Caucasus with Shi'i majority.
1996	Taliban seize Kabul and gain control over much of Afghanistan, imposing strict Sharia law.
2001	September 11—Muslim extremist group Al-Qaeda, led by Osama bin Laden, launches major terrorist attack on United States in New York and Washington. Leads to U.S.-headed invasion of Afghanistan and downfall of Taliban. Al-Qaeda leadership is dispersed.
2003	Coalition led by the U.S. invades Iraq and topples head of state Saddam Hussein.

Key Figures and Dynasties in Islamic History

All dates are A.D.

Abbasids—Dynasty founded by Abu al-Abbas al-Sattah, which toppled the Umayyads in Damascus. The Abbasids transferred the Caliphate to Baghdad. The family continued to fill the Caliph role well after they had lost their political power. Based their legitimacy on claims of descent from Muhammad's uncle Abbas.

Abu Bakr (570-634)—The first Caliph and father of Aisha, wife of the Prophet Muhammad. He was a merchant and reputedly the first male convert to Islam (the women of Muhammad's household being the very first). He was a close friend of Muhammad and was buried beside him.

Aisha (614-678)—The daughter of Abu Bakr and the third and favorite wife of Muhammad. She was literate, noted especially for her eloquence and knowledge of poetry.

Akbar—One of the great Mughal emperors, his reign was characterized by a tolerant attitude towards religion. His favorable policies towards the Hindu population were reversed by his descendants.

Ali—Cousin of Muhammad and son of Abu Talib. He married Muhammad's favorite daughter, Fatima, and married no one else while Muhammad lived. One of the first converts to Islam, he also became the fourth Caliph. He fought Muhammad's widow Aisha for the Caliphate at the Battle of the Camel (656), and was killed in 660 while still in power, albeit with drastically diminished authority.

Aurangzeb (1618–1707)—Mughal emperor who actively sought to impose Muslim orthodoxy after the lax approach adopted by his ancestor Akbar and subsequent emperors. His reforms led to heightened tensions between the Muslims and the majority Hindu population.

Ayatollah Khomeini—Charismatic religious leader who, from exile in Paris, sparked revolution in Iran and the downfall of the Shah in 1979. Established leadership of the Shi'i clergy and imposed strict Islamic laws. He took up a vociferously anti-American stance.

Ayyubids—Dynasty established by Saladin, ruled Egypt from 1171-1250 and was responsible for restoring Sunnism to Egypt after the lengthy rule of the Shi'i Fatimids.

Babur (1483-1530)—Founder of the Mughal dynasty in India. Of Turkic/Mongol origins. A descendant of Genghis Khan on his mother's side and Timur on his father's.

Fatima—The favourite daughter of Muhammad and Khadija, whose life in particular has been woven with many legends. She was married to Ali, and was the mother of the Shi'i saints Hasan and Husayn. She died six months after the Prophet's death.

Fatimids—Dynasty, originating in Tunisia, which ruled in Egypt from 969 to 1171. Adherents of Shi'ism, they were the major rivals of the Abbasid Caliphate.

Husayn (*c.*626–680)—Second son of Caliph Ali and Fatima, daughter of Muhammad. He was killed at Karbala at the hands of the Umayyads whilst attempting to regain the Caliphate for his family line—an event that is commemorated during Ashura, the most important religious festival in the Shi'i calendar.

Hulegu—Mongol leader, grandson of Genghis Khan, who established the Il-Khan Empire in Iran/Iraq. Destroyed Baghdad in 1258 and had the ruling Caliph and his family killed.

Ibn Battuta—An indefatigably adventurous judge who traveled some 75,000 miles on numerous journeys from West Africa to China, India and the Russian Steppes in the fourteenth century. His account of his travels remains a fascinating and valuable historical document, unparalleled in the medieval world.

Ibn Khaldun (1332-1406)—Enormously influential thinker, born in Tunis (in Tunisia) and died in Cairo. His *Muqaddima* (Introduction) to his *Universal History* brings together a wide variety of topics to elaborate a theory of world history that has been hailed as the first comprehensive critical study of the subject.

Ibn Sina (980-1037)—Known in the West as Avicenna. A major figure in Islamic scholarship especially famous for his *Medical Canon*. Translated into Latin, it was used as standard work of reference in European medical colleges until the seventeenth century.

Ibn Tulun—Governor of Egypt who broke away from Abbasid control and established near-independent rule in Egypt between 868 and 905.

Ismail—Founder of the Persian Safavid dynasty. Ismail imposed Shi'ism as the state religion, helping to create the distinctive Shi'i identity in Iran today.

Khadija (556-619)—The first wife of Muhammad. She is said to have been married twice before. A woman of property, she was considerably older than Muhammad, although they had several children, including Zainab, Umm Kulthum, Fatima, and Ruqayya. She supported and encouraged Muhammad, and died in 619, to his immense grief. He married no other woman while she was alive.

Kharijis—The smallest of the three branches of Islam, today counting for less than one percent of all Muslims. The Kharijis broke with the majority of Muslims in 658 over the succession to the Caliphate, and have both extremist and moderate branches.

Mu'awiya—Founder of the Umayyad dynasty and responsible for making the role of Caliph hereditary.

Mughals—Muslim dynasty founded in 1658 by Babur, and which remained in power until it was dismantled by the British two centuries later.

Muhammad—The Prophet and founder of Islam, known as the Messenger of God, and through whom the Qur'an was revealed. He was born into a poor family of good blood (his father Abdullah was a merchant) in Mecca between 570 and 580, orphaned at an early age, and died in 632. His calling to prophethood came late in life.

Ottomans—Turkish dynasty founded in Anatolia, with Istanbul (Constantinople) as its capital, thereby putting an end to a thousand years of Christian Byzantine history in the region. The Ottomans went on to rule an empire of enormous breadth and diversity. The Ottomans posed a continuous threat to Western Europe, yet ultimately failed to keep up with the rapid pace of European modernization and went into decline. Eventually dismantled by the Allies after siding with Germany during World War I.

Quraysh—The dominant Arab tribe in Mecca to which Muhammad belonged.

Safavids—Dynasty founded by Ismail in 1501. Imposed Shi'ism as the state religion and pursued wars against its great Sunni rivals, the Ottoman Empire.

Saladin (1138-1193)—Sultan of Egypt and one of the greatest heroes in the Islamic world. He led successful campaigns against the Crusaders and reclaimed Jerusalem for the Muslims. Established the Ayyubid dynasty in Egypt (r. 1171-1250) and restored Sunnism to Egypt after the lengthy rule of the Shi'i Fatimids.

Shah Jahan (1592-166)—Mughal emperor of India whose rule (1628-58) marks the Golden Age of Mugal art and architecture, exemplified by the Taj Majal monument constructed in Agra.

Sulayman the Magnificent (1494-1566)—Ottoman Sultan who strengthened and expanded the Ottoman Empire.

Tariq—The Berber general whose army defeated the Visigoths in Spain in 711 and introduced Islamic rule to the Iberian Peninsula. The Rock of Gibraltar, meaning "Tariq's Rock," is named after him.

Timur (1336-1405)—Known in English as Tamerlane, the descendant of Genghis Khan established the great Mongol dynasties through his conquests.

Umar (*d.* 640)—The second Caliph. Like St. Paul, he was at first a vociferous opponent of the Muslims but he finally converted and defended Islam with the same zeal he had used to attack it. He married Muhammad's daughter Hafsa.

Umayyads—Dynasty founded by the Caliph Mu'awiya in 661. They ruled over the period of the greatest Muslim expansion from their capital at Damascus, Syria. It was Mu'awiya who controversially made the position of Caliph hereditary. Deposed by the Abbasids in 750.

Uthman (*r.* 644-56)—The third Caliph and one of the first converts to Islam. He was originally a rich merchant who married Muhammad's daughter Ruqayya.

Wahhabi (*c.* 1703-1791)—Highly influential eighteenth-century thinker and founder of an Islamic revival movement which openly challenged the Ottoman authorities. Wahhabi was responsible for converting the Saud tribe of central Arabia which during the nineteenth century waged major military campaigns in the region, seriously undermining Ottoman control.

Glossary of Islamic Terms

adhan (*ādhān* آذان)—the call to prayer.

Al-Azhar—prestigious mosque and teaching institution in Cairo. Considered the oldest university in the world still in existence.

Ansar (*al-anṣār* الأنصار)—the "Helpers," the citizens in Medina who supported Muhammad after his flight from Mecca.

burqa (*burqa* برقة)—a veil, generally of black cloth, that covers the whole head, limbs and body of a woman for purposes of modesty. Also spelled **burka** and **burkha**.

Caliph (*khalīfa* خليفة)—a Muslim ruler.

dhimmi—person belonging to a protected minority, principally Jewish or Christian but by extension one of a number of other recognized non-Islamic religions, who lives under Muslim rule.

fatwa (*fatwa* فتوة)—legal verdict based on the Qur'an and the Sunna, which are the recorded sayings and deeds of Muhammad.

fiqh (*fiqh* فقه)—religious law.

Hadith (*ḥadīth* حديث)—the sayings and deeds of the prophet Muhammad recorded by his followers. Considered authoritative and perfect. A saying is called a **sunna**, hence "Sunni" Islam.

Hajar (*ḥajar* حجر)—the Black Stone set into the corner of the Ka'aba in Mecca. Tradition states it fell from heaven.

hajj (*ḥajj* حج)—the pilgrimage to Mecca which is required of all Muslims once in a lifetime. One of the five pillars of Islam.

hajji (*ḥājj* حاج)—the title given to someone who has made the pilgrimage to Mecca.

hijab (*ḥijāb* هجاب)—a large headscarf that serves as a veil to cover the head and hair of a woman for purposes of modesty. Also spelled **hejab**.

Hijra (*hijra* هجرة)—Muhammad's immigration to Medina. It begins the Muslim calendar.

Hudud (*ḥudūd* حدود)—selected Islamic laws governing morality, including matters of dress, adultery, theft, and even television-watching in Afghanistan. These are not considered binding by most Muslims, but countries such as Saudi Arabia, Sudan, and Northern Nigeria use these laws to bolster their own interpretations of Islamic law.

Iblis (*iblīs* إبليس)—Satan. Also known as **Shaitan**.

imam (*imām* إمام)—a religious leader. Also a name commonly used by Shi'is for their political leaders in place of Caliph. Also known as a **mullah** or **mollah** (*mullah* ملة).

Injil (*al-injīl* الإنجيل)—the Gospels or New Testament.

Islam (*al-islām* الإسلام)—submission, the religion of all the prophets of Allah culminating in the Prophet Muhammad.

Janna (*al-janna* الجنة)—the heavenly garden, Paradise. The place of the faithful in the afterlife.

jihad (*jihād* جهاد)—holy war.

Ka'aba (*al-ka'ba* الكعبة)—a cube-shaped building in Mecca containing a stone laid there by Abraham and Ishmael. All Muslims face the Ka'aba when praying.

Qur'an (*al-qur'ān al-karīm* القرآن الكريم)—also spelled **Koran**. The holy book of Islam given to Muhammad by Allah through the Archangel Gabriel. "Qur'an" literally means "the recital." It is the final revelation of Allah given to the prophet Muhammad. It has 114 suras, or chapters, arranged in order of length.

madrasa (*madrasa* مدرسة)—teaching mosques, or religious colleges, the key educational institutions in Islam.

masjid (*masjid* مسجد)—mosque.

Mecca (*makka* مكة)—the Holy City of Islam. It is the birthplace of Muhammad.

Medina (*al-madīna* المدينة)—The city, formerly called Yathrib, that Muhammad fled to after announcing Islam. The name stands for "City of the Prophet."

muhajir (*muhājir* مهاجر)—"emigrant," one who leaves his home town to join a Muslim community.

Nasara (*naṣārā* نصارى)—a word used in the Qur'an to designate those who are Christians.

qadi *or* **qazi** (*qāḍi* قاض)—an Islamic judge.

qibla (*qibla* قبلة)—the direction in which Muslims turn for daily prayers, towards Mecca.

Ramadan (*ramadān* رمضان)—the ninth month of the Islamic calendar which is the month of the fast.

sala or **salaat** (*salāh* صلاة)—prayers. One of the Five Pillars of Islam.

sawm (*sawm* صوم)—fasting, usually during Ramadan. One of the Five Pillars of Islam.

Shi'ism (*ash-shī'a* الشيعة)—major rival Islamic sect to the majority orthodox Sunnis. They maintain their own leaders and emphasized the primacy of Ali, rejecting the line of Sunni Caliphs. Shi'is account for perhaps ten percent of all Muslims today.

sufism (*taṣawwuf* تصوف)—a sect of Islam. It is very mystical and teaches strong self-denial with the hope of union with God.

sunna (*as-sunna* السنة)—the life, practices, and sayings of Muhammad recorded as examples of perfect conduct in society, religion, action, etc. They contain the **Hadiths**.

Sunnism (*ahl as-sunna* أهل السنة)—the main sect of Islam, commonly held to be "orthodox." Sunnis make up almost ninety percent of the international Islamic community.

sura (*sūra* سورة)—a chapter of the Qur'an.

taqiya (*taqiyya* تقية)—the Shi'i doctrine that permits believers to pretend they are not Muslim when under duress or threat to their safety.

tawhid (*tawḥīd* توحيد)—the belief that there is only one God.

Tawra (*at-tawrāh* التوراة)—the Torah or Old Testament.

Ulema (*'ulamā'* علماء)—religious scholars or clerics.

umma (*umma* أمة)—a religious community, usually referring to an Islamic one.

zakat (*zakāh* زكاة)—the third pillar of Islam: giving alms, charity that is given to the poor.

Index

215

Index

Index

Illustrated Histories from Hippocrene Books

Each of these volumes depicts the entire history of a region or people, from earliest times to the present. Fifty handsome black-and-white illustrations, maps, and photographs complement each book. Written in an accessible, engaging style, they are ideal for students, inquisitive travelers, and anyone interested in the heritage of a particular nation or people!

CITIES

Cracow: An Illustrated History
Zdislaw Zygulski, Jr.
160 pages • 5 x 7 • 60 photos/illus./maps • ISBN 0-7818-0837-5 • W • $12.95pb • (154)

London: An Illustrated History
Robert Chester & Nicholas Awde
224 pages • 5 x 7 • 360 b/w photos/illus./maps • ISBN 0-7818-0908-8 • W • $12.95pb • (300)

Moscow: An Illustrated History
Kathleen Berton Murrell
250 pages • 5 x 7 • 50 b/w photos/illus./maps • ISBN 0-7818-0945-2 • W • $14.95pb • (419)

Paris: An Illustrated History
Elaine Mokhtefi
182 pages • 5 x 7 • 50 b/w photos/illus./maps • ISBN 0-7818-0838-3 • W • $12.95pb • (136)

CIVILIZATIONS

The Arab World: An Illustrated History
Kirk Sowell
200 pages • 5 1/2 x 8 1/2 • 50 b/w photos/illus./maps • ISBN 0-7818-0990-8 • W • $14.95pb • (465)

The Celtic World: An Illustrated History
Patrick Lavin
185 pages • 5 x 7 • 50 b/w photos/illus./maps • ISBN 0-7818-0731-X • W • $14.95hc • (582)
185 pages • 5 x 7 • 50 b/w photos/illus./maps • ISBN 0-7818-1005-1 • W • $12.95pb • (478)

COUNTRIES

China: An Illustrated History
Yong Ho
142 pages • 5 x 7 • 50 b/w photos/illus./maps • ISBN 0-7818-0821-9 • W • $14.95hc • (542)

Egypt: An Illustrated History
Fred James Hill
160 pages • 5 x 7 • 65 b/w photos/illus./maps • ISBN 0-7818-0911-8 • W • $12.95pb • (311)

England: An Illustrated History
Henry Weisser
166 pages • 5 x 7 • 50 b/w photos/illus./maps • ISBN 0-7818-0751-4 • W • $11.95hc • (446)

France: An Illustrated History
Lisa Neal
150 pages • 5 x 7 • 50 b/w photos/illus./maps • ISBN 0-7818-0835-9 • W • $14.95hc • (105)
150 pages • 5 x 7 • 50 b/w photos/illus./maps • ISBN 0-7818-0872-3 • W • $12.95pb • (340)

Greece: An Illustrated History
Tom Stone
180 pages • 5 x 7 • 50 b/w photos/illus./maps • ISBN 0-7818-0755-7 • W • $14.95hc • (557)

India: An Illustrated History
Prem Kishore & Anuradha Kishore Ganpati
224 pages • 5 x 7 • 50 b/w photos/illus./maps • ISBN 0-7818-0944-4 • W • $14.95pb • (424)

Ireland: An Illustrated History
Henry Weisser
166 pages • 5 x 7 • 50 b/w photos/illus./maps • ISBN 0-7818-0693-3 • W • $11.95hc • (782)

Israel: An Illustrated History
David C. Gross
160 pages • 5 x 7 • 50 b/w photos/illus./maps • ISBN 0-7818-0756-5 • W • $11.95hc • (24)

Italy: An Illustrated History
Joseph F. Privitera
142 pages • 5 x 7 • 50 b/w photos/illus./maps • ISBN 0-7818-0819-7 • W • $14.95hc • (436)

Japan: An Illustrated History
Shelton Woods
200 pages • 5 x 7 • 50 b/w photos/illus./maps • ISBN 0-7818-0989-4 • W • $14.95pb • (469)

Korea: An Illustrated History from Ancient Times to 1945
David Rees
154 pages • 5 x 7 • 50 b/w photos/illus./maps • ISBN 0-7818-0873-1 • W • $12.95pb • (354)

Mexico: An Illustrated History
Michael Burke
180 pages • 5 x 7 • 50 b/w photos/illus./maps • ISBN 0-7818-0690-9 • W • $11.95hc • (585)

Poland: An Illustrated History
Iwo Cyprian Pogonowski
272 pages • 5 x 7 • 50 b/w photos/illus./maps • ISBN 0-7818-0757-3 • W • $16.95hc • (404)

Poland in World War II: An Illustrated Military History
Andrew Hempel
120 pages • 5 x 7 • 50 b/w photos/illus./maps • ISBN 0-7818-0758-1 • W • $11.95hc • (541)
120 pages • 5 x 7 • 50 b/w photos/illus./maps • ISBN 0-7818-1004-3 • W • $9.95pb • (484)

Romania: An Illustrated History
Nicolae Klepper
298 pages • 5 x 7 • 50 b/w photos/illus./maps • ISBN 0-7818-0935-5 • W • $14.95pb • (366)

Russia: An Illustrated History
Joel Carmichael
252 pages • 5 x 7 • 50 b/w photos/illus./maps • ISBN 0-7818-0689-5 • W • $14.95hc • (781)

Sicily: An Illustrated History
Joseph F. Privitera
152 pages • 5 x 7 • 50 b/w photos/illus./maps • ISBN 0-7818-0909-6 • W • $12.95pb • (301)

Spain: An Illustrated History
Fred James Hill
176 pages • 5 x 7 • 50 b/w photos/illus./maps • ISBN 0-7818-0874-X • W • $12.95pb • (339)

Tikal: An Illustrated History of the Ancient Maya Capital
John Montgomery
274 pages • 6 x 9 • 50 b/w photos/illus./maps • ISBN 0-7818-0853-7 • W • $14.95pb • (101)

Vietnam: An Illustrated History
Shelton Woods
172 pages • 5 x 7 • 50 b/w photos/illus./maps • ISBN 0-7818-0910-X • W • $14.95pb • (302)

Wales: An Illustrated History
Henry Weisser
228 pages • 5 x 7 • 50 b/w photos/illus./maps • ISBN 0-7818-0936-3 • W • $12.95pb • (418)

STATES

Arizona: An Illustrated History
Patrick Lavin
250 pages • 5 x 7 • 65 b/w photos/illus. maps • ISBN 0-7818-0852-9 • W • $14.95pb • (102)